good for you!
fast and healthy family favorites

WILEY

WILEY PUBLISHING, INC.

For general information on our other products and services for technical support
please contact our Customer Care Department within the U.S. at 800-762-2974,
outside the U.S. at 317-572-3993 or fax 317-572-4002.

Wiley also publishes its books in a variety of electronic formats. Some content that
appears in print may not be available in electronic books. For more information about
Wiley products, visit our web site at www.wiley.com.

Library of Congress Cataloging-in-Publication Data:

Pillsbury good for you : fast and healthy family favorites / Pillsbury editors.
    p. cm.
  Includes index.
ISBN-13: 978-0-7645-9724-4
ISBN-10: 0-7645-9724-8 (cloth)
1. Quick and easy cookery. 2. Low-fat diet--Recipes. I. Title: Good for you. II.
C.A. Pillsbury and Company.
  TX833.5.P554 2006
  641.5'55--dc22

                                              2005032311

Manufactured in China

10 9 8 7 6 5 4 3 2 1

Cover photo: Lemon-basil skillet chicken with rice (page 130)
Title page photo: Fast fajita and vegetable pita (page 46)
Photo on page 6: Ariel Skelley/Getty Images; Photo on page 8: ©2006
Imagine/JupiterImages Corporation; photo on page 10: Photodisc/Getty Images, Inc.;
Photo on page 11: John Henry/Getty Images, Inc.

General Mills

Director, Book and Online Publishing:
Kim Walter

Manager, Book Publishing:
Lois Tlusty

Editor:
Cheri Olerud

Recipe Development and Testing:
Pillsbury Kitchens

Photography:
General Mills Photography Studios
and Image Library

Photographer:
Val Bourassa

Food Stylists:
Carol Grones and Susan Brue

Wiley Publishing, Inc.

Publisher:
Natalie Chapman

Executive Editor:
Anne Ficklen

Editor:
Kristi Hart

Production Editor:
Leslie Anglin

Cover Design:
Suzanne Sunwoo

Interior Design and Layout:
Lee Goldstein

Photography Art Direction:
Paul DiNovo

Manufacturing Manager:
Kevin Watt

*Our recipes have been
tested in the Pillsbury Kitchens
and meet our standards of easy
preparation, reliability and great taste.*

For more great recipes, visit pillsbury.com

from the pillsbury kitchens
home of the pillsbury
bake-off® contest

Welcome . . .

Want to feed your family great-tasting, nutritious meals but think you don't have enough time or know-how to do it? Think again! You'll be surprised how easy this book makes it to incorporate healthy eating into your fast-paced lifestyle.

Right up front is a practical guide that gives you the simple keys to good health, plus ways to make over your shopping list with better-for-you choices and how to get your family to "think healthy." Then, throughout the book, families just like yours share their own tips and experiences in meeting the fast-and-healthy dinner challenge.

All 170 recipes follow those guidelines, plus they're fast, easy to make and use everyday ingredients. You can make any recipe in just 4 or 5 steps and 30 minutes or less, and Superfast recipes are ready in 20 minutes or less. From easy breakfast and 5-ingredient dinners to on-the-go dinners and dinners on the grill, this book is indispensable to healthy, busy families.

So relax. What's good for you is also easy and delicious!

The Pillsbury Editors

contents

fast and healthy dinners

the challenge: *fast, healthy dinners*

"Dinner is definitely a crunch time. I want to make a healthy dinner for my family, but with both of us gone all day and the kids busy with homework, sports and music, it's just not possible on most school nights."

the solution: *2 easy steps*

Make your dinnertime dream real with these easy steps.

step 1. *eat dinner together*

If your family eats dinner together most evenings of the week, you already have a solid foundation and are well on your way to healthy eating.

Families who eat together consume more fruits and vegetables, fiber, vitamins and minerals and less fat.

The dinner table shapes good eating habits that have a lasting impact, and homemade meals tend to be more wholesome than take-out or restaurant foods.

step 2. *choose fast and healthy recipes*

The recipes in this cookbook are perfect for time-pressed families like yours—they taste great, are fast, healthy and easy, and use every-day ingredients. They also:

➤ contain fruits, vegetables, beans and whole grains laden with fiber, Vitamins A and C, calcium and iron

➤ call for canola, soybean and olive oils that are heart-healthy, good fats for stir-frying and cooking

➤ use fat-free skim milk, reduced-fat cheese, reduced-fat or fat-free cream cheese and sour cream

➤ take 20 to 30 minutes to prepare

➤ many require only five ingredients

➤ many can be taken on-the-go

5 *simple ways*
to eat healthier

These five actions are key to good health.

➤ **1.** *eat more fruits and vegetables*

Eating five to nine servings of fruits and vegetables every day ensures that you get enough Vitamins A and C and folic acid, all necessary nutrients for a healthy body. For added convenience, use frozen and canned fruits and vegetables—they are as nutritious as their fresh counterparts.

➤ **2.** *choose whole grains and foods high in fiber*

Eat whole grain breads and cereals from oats, wheat, rice and corn and other grains. Eating whole grains protects against heart disease, diabetes and certain cancers. Fiber keeps foods moving through your digestive tract. To increase your fiber, eat more beans and bran, and look for foods that contain at least 3 grams of fiber.

➤ **3.** *eat foods moderate in fat and cholesterol*

Reducing fat, especially saturated fat, and cholesterol matters. Replacing high-fat meats with lean cuts and low-fat substitutes, like using turkey kielbasa instead of pork kielbasa and using sirloin steak instead of stew meat in stew, makes a big difference in lowering fat. Instead of using butter or margarine for stir-frying and skillet dishes, use canola, soybean or olive oil. Increase your consumption of beans, and eat less meat overall.

➤ **4.** *prepare foods with less salt and sugar*

Find ways to cut down on salt (sodium) and sugar. When cooking pasta, omit salt in the cooking water and cut down on chips and crackers. Canned beans and vegetables are convenient and nutritious, but contain sodium—you can rinse them to reduce the sodium. To reduce sugar, eat less candy and baked goods like cake, doughnuts and muffins and drink less soda.

➤ **5.** *be active every day*

Try to devote 30 to 60 minutes most days to whatever activity you enjoy: walking, running, swimming or biking. Being active helps maintain weight, prevent disease and promote positive mental health. It's important for your children to see you being active, and for the kids to be active, too. Get together and go for a walk, play a game of tag, kick the soccer ball or let the kids choose.

shopping list
makeover

Now's the time to update your grocery list! Replace the good old standards with better-for-you choices that provide more nutrients and less fat, salt or sugar.

Before ➤➤➤ After

MEAT
pork sausage

75% lean
    ground beef
chicken pieces
pork chops

MEAT
low-fat turkey sausage

85-90% lean
    ground beef
skinless chicken breasts
lean pork chops

DELI
ham

fried chicken

DELI
extra-lean turkey
    or roast beef
rotisserie chicken

DAIRY
Cheddar cheese
regular or 2% milk
sour cream

flour tortillas
butter or margarine

DAIRY
reduced-fat Cheddar cheese
1% or fat-free (skim) milk
reduced-fat sour cream
    or fat-free yogurt
whole wheat tortillas
canola, soybean or olive oil

CONDIMENTS
ketchup
mayonnaise
salt
oil

CONDIMENTS
salsa or picante sauce
reduced-fat mayonnaise
spice and herb blends
cooking spray

Before ➤➤➤ After

CANNED FOODS
fruit packed in
    heavy syrup
cream soups
refried beans
pork and beans

CANNED FOODS
fruit packed in juice

broth or clear soups
fat-free refried beans
vegetarian baked beans

BAKERY
white bread
doughnuts
cinnamon rolls

BAKERY
whole-grain breads
bagels
cinnamon-raisin bread

FROZEN FOODS
sweetened grape juice
vegetables in sauce
ice cream
pops on a stick

FROZEN FOODS
100% fruit juice blend
plain vegetables
low-fat frozen yogurt
fruit juice bars

SNACK FOODS
potato chips
tortilla chips
sour cream dip
soda pop

SNACK FOODS
pretzels or pretzel chips
baked tortilla chips
bean or salsa dip
flavored sparkling water

CEREALS
flavored instant oatmeal
granola

CEREALS
old-fashioned oatmeal
low-fat granola

20 quick ways to better nutrition for your family

Try these sure-fire ways to get the family to "think healthy."

1. Add vegetables and beans to soups, stews and casseroles.

2. Encourage family members to keep a bottle of water with them to drink from during the day.

3. Grocery shop from a list to limit high-calorie snacks and foods.

4. Stock your pantry with whole wheat pasta, brown rice, canned beans for quick prep.

5. Use canned and frozen fruits and vegetables if that's what your family likes. They contain just as many vitamins and minerals as the fresh ones.

6. Aim for small, gradual improvements in your family's eating habits.

7. Keep low-fat yogurt, cheese, nuts and other healthy snacks handy for the kids.

8. Eat a breakfast cereal with at least 5 grams of fiber.

9. Spice up the taste of low-fat foods with fresh herbs added near the end of cook time.

10. Find an activity (or two) that you and your family can enjoy together and be active at least 30 minutes every day.

11. Spend at least 15 minutes enjoying each meal.

12. Rinse browned ground beef under hot water before using in soups or casseroles.

13. Top popcorn with grated Parmesan cheese or spice or herb blend instead of butter.

14. Keep an eye on portion sizes. Compare the serving size on food labels to what family members actually eat.

15. Bring a fruit or vegetable platter with low-fat dip to potlucks or gatherings.

16. Serve your families' favorite foods. Just cut down on the amount and how often you serve them.

17. Try salsa, flavored mustards or low-fat salad dressings in place of mayonnaise.

18. Add skim milk and a green vegetable, salad or fruit to round out a meal.

19. Find restaurants that offer nutrition information and choices, so your family can still eat out and eat healthy.

20. Relax and reflect on the positive changes you and your family have made.

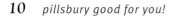

12 easy ways to sneak in
veggies and fruits

To get them to eat veggies and fruits, let the kids:

➤ **1.** Snack on cut-up carrots, celery, cucumbers or grape tomatoes.

➤ **2.** Dunk veggies into a favorite low-fat dressing.

➤ **3.** "Play" with their food. Cut carrots and celery into coins, broccoli and cauliflower into trees and forests.

➤ **4.** Load sandwiches with sliced cucumbers, tomatoes, onions, bell peppers, zucchini or other vegetables.

➤ **5.** Toss pasta with their favorites—corn, peas, green beans or carrots—before topping with sauce.

➤ **6.** Enjoy ketchup, tomato and pasta sauces and tomato soup—they count.

➤ **7.** Eat veggies yourself.

➤ **8.** Layer a parfait with strawberries, cereal and yogurt.

➤ **9.** Blend a smoothie using chopped fresh fruit, ice and fat-free yogurt.

➤ **10.** Top cereal, pancakes, waffles and French toast with fruit.

➤ **11.** Freeze grapes, strawberries and banana chunks and eat.

➤ **12.** Snack on dried raisins, dates, peaches and apricots.

chapter 1

easy breakfast dinners

"*My kids love breakfast, and I never have time to cook in the morning before work. Serving breakfast for dinner would be perfect.*"

—*Lisa P.*

SUPER EXPRESS *Ready in 20 minutes or less*

apple–canadian bacon omelet SUPER EXPRESS

start to finish / **20 MINUTES**

4 servings

"*I love the taste of butter and as long as I eat just a little, it's okay once in a while. Just a bit of butter packs lots of flavor and makes this smoky Canadian bacon and sweet apple omelet a great dinner for my family.*"

—Andi

4 teaspoons butter or margarine

2 medium Golden Delicious apples, peeled, cut into thin wedges (about 2 cups)

4 oz. Canadian bacon (about 6 slices), cut into thin strips

2 tablespoons real maple syrup

1 1/2 cups fat-free cholesterol-free egg product (from two 8-oz. cartons) or 4 whole eggs plus 4 egg whites, lightly beaten

1/8 teaspoon pepper

1. In 8-inch nonstick skillet or 2-quart saucepan, melt 1 teaspoon of the butter over medium heat. Add apple; cook about 5 minutes, stirring occasionally, until crisp-tender. Stir in Canadian bacon. Reduce heat to medium-low; cook and stir about 2 minutes. Remove from heat. Stir in syrup.

2. Meanwhile, in medium bowl, mix egg product or beaten eggs and egg whites and the pepper until well blended.

3. In 10-inch nonstick skillet with flared sides (omelet pan), melt remaining 3 teaspoons butter over medium heat. Pour egg mixture into skillet. Cook about 1 minute, lifting edges occasionally to allow uncooked egg mixture to flow to bottom of skillet, until mixture begins to cook around edges. Reduce heat to medium-low; cover and cook 3 to 6 minutes or until set.

4. Spoon half of filling over half of omelet; quickly fold other half of omelet over filling. Cut omelet in half; slide each half onto serving plate. Spoon remaining filling over each serving.

1 Serving: Calories 210 (Calories from Fat 60); Total Fat 6g (Saturated Fat 3g; Trans Fat 0g); Cholesterol 25mg; Sodium 680mg; Total Carbohydrate 19g (Dietary Fiber 2g; Sugars 15g); Protein 19g
% Daily Value: Vitamin A 15%; Vitamin C 2%; Calcium 4%; Iron 15%
Exchanges: 1/2 Fruit, 1/2 Other Carbohydrate, 2 1/2 Very Lean Meat, 1 Fat
Carbohydrate Choices: 1

apple–canadian bacon omelet

spinach and bacon
omelet SUPER EXPRESS

start to finish **/ 15 MINUTES**

4 servings

**1 1/2 cups fat-free cholesterol-free egg product (from two 8-oz. cartons) or
4 whole eggs plus 4 egg whites, lightly beaten**

1/4 cup plus 2 tablespoons water

1/4 teaspoon pepper

2 tablespoons real bacon pieces

1 cup chopped fresh spinach

1/4 cup finely shredded Parmesan cheese

1. In medium bowl, mix egg product, the water and pepper until well blended. Stir in bacon.

2. Heat 10-inch nonstick skillet with flared sides (omelet pan) over medium-high heat. Reduce heat to medium; spread spinach in skillet. Pour egg mixture over spinach. Cook about 1 minute, lifting edges occasionally to allow uncooked egg mixture to flow to bottom of skillet, until mixture begins to cook around edges. Reduce heat to medium-low; cover and cook 3 to 6 minutes or until set.

3. Sprinkle Parmesan cheese over half of omelet; fold other half of omelet over filling. Cut omelet in half; slide each half onto serving plate.

1 Serving: Calories 100 (Calories from Fat 30); Total Fat 3g (Saturated Fat 1.5g; Trans Fat 0g); Cholesterol 5mg; Sodium 370mg; Total Carbohydrate 3g (Dietary Fiber 1g; Sugars 1g); Protein 15g
% Daily Value: Vitamin A 25%; Vitamin C 0%; Calcium 15%; Iron 15%
Exchanges: 2 Very Lean Meat, 1/2 Fat
Carbohydrate Choices: 0

egg and cheese
burritos SUPER EXPRESS

start to finish / **10 MINUTES**

4 burritos

"I watch the amount of cholesterol in the foods and recipes our family eats. If it's over 150 milligrams cholesterol per serving, I use an egg substitute, and my kids don't know the difference."
—Cheri

4 flour tortillas (8 to 10 inch)
1 teaspoon olive or canola oil
2 cups fat-free cholesterol-free egg product (from two 8-oz. cartons) or
   8 eggs, lightly beaten
1/4 cup shredded reduced-fat Cheddar cheese (1 oz.)
1/2 cup chunky-style salsa

1. Heat tortillas as directed on package; keep warm.

2. Meanwhile, in 10-inch nonstick skillet, heat oil over medium-high heat. Pour egg product into skillet; cook, stirring frequently, until set. Sprinkle cheese over egg product; let stand until melted.

3. Spoon egg mixture evenly onto warm tortillas. Top each with salsa. Roll up tortillas.

1 Burrito: Calories 220 (Calories from Fat 45); Total Fat 5g (Saturated Fat 1g; Trans Fat 0g); Cholesterol 0mg; Sodium 630mg; Total Carbohydrate 28g (Dietary Fiber 3g; Sugars 3g); Protein 18g
% Daily Value: Vitamin A 15%; Vitamin C 4%; Calcium 15%; Iron 20%
Exchanges: 1 Starch, 1 Other Carbohydrate, 2 Very Lean Meat, 1/2 Fat
Carbohydrate Choices: 2

tortilla
eggs SUPER EXPRESS

4 servings

"Not only are canola and olive oils better for me and my family, they also make my favorite recipes taste great."

—Kelly

1 teaspoon olive or canola oil

1 medium green bell pepper, chopped (1 cup)

2 medium onions, chopped (1 cup)

1 3/4 cups fat-free cholesterol-free egg product (from two 8-oz. cartons) or 6 whole eggs plus 2 egg whites, lightly beaten

1/3 cup fat-free (skim) milk

1/2 teaspoon salt

1/8 teaspoon pepper

4 fat-free flour tortillas (10 inch)

1/2 cup shredded nonfat Cheddar cheese (2 oz.)

1/4 cup chunky-style salsa

1. In 10-inch nonstick skillet, heat oil over medium heat. Add bell pepper and onions; cover and cook 4 to 6 minutes, stirring occasionally, until tender.

2. In medium bowl, mix egg product, milk, salt and pepper until well blended. Pour egg product mixture over vegetables; cook until set, occasionally stirring gently.

   Meanwhile, heat tortillas as directed on package. Place warm tortillas on individual plates.

3. Spoon scrambled egg mixture down center of each tortilla. Top each with cheese and salsa. Roll up tortillas.

1 Serving: Calories 260 (Calories from Fat 40); Total Fat 4.5g (Saturated Fat 1g; Trans Fat 0g); Cholesterol 0mg; Sodium 660mg; Total Carbohydrate 36g (Dietary Fiber 4g; Sugars 8g); Protein 21g
% Daily Value: Vitamin A 20%; Vitamin C 30%; Calcium 25%; Iron 20%
Exchanges: 2 Starch, 1/2 Other Carbohydrate, 2 Very Lean Meat
Carbohydrate Choices: 2 1/2

egg and ham
roll-ups SUPER EXPRESS

start to finish **/ 20 MINUTES**

4 servings

1 1/2 cups fat-free cholesterol-free egg product (from two 8-oz. cartons) or
    6 eggs, lightly beaten
1/8 teaspoon pepper
1 teaspoon canola or soybean oil
1/4 cup fat-free cream cheese (from 8-oz. container)
1/4 cup no-sugar-added all-fruit strawberry spread
4 fat-free flour tortillas (8 to 10 inch)
1/4 lb. sliced cooked reduced-fat ham (from deli)

1. Heat oven to 400°F. In small bowl, mix egg product and pepper until well blended. In 8-inch nonstick skillet, heat oil over medium heat. Reduce heat to medium-low. Pour egg product mixture into skillet; cook, stirring constantly, until set but still moist. Remove from heat.

2. In another small bowl, mix cream cheese and strawberry spread (mixture will be lumpy). Spread 2 tablespoons mixture over each tortilla.

3. Down center 1/3 of each tortilla, place 1/4 of ham slices and scrambled egg product. Fold sides of tortillas over filling. Place folded side down on ungreased cookie sheet.

4. Bake 3 to 5 minutes or until thoroughly heated.

1 Serving: Calories 330 (Calories from Fat 100); Total Fat 11g (Saturated Fat 4.5g; Trans Fat 0.5g); Cholesterol 30mg; Sodium 750mg; Total Carbohydrate 38g (Dietary Fiber 3g; Sugars 12g); Protein 20g
% Daily Value: Vitamin A 15%; Vitamin C 0%; Calcium 10%; Iron 20%
Exchanges: 1 1/2 Starch, 1 Other Carbohydrate, 2 Very Lean Meat, 2 Fat
Carbohydrate Choices: 2 1/2

scrambled egg and veggie pockets SUPER EXPRESS

start to finish / **20 MINUTES**

4 sandwiches

"The veggies add lots of crunch and lots of vitamins and minerals to this easy, colorful dinner. It's good to know I can use my family's favorite veggies or any veggies I have on hand."
—Karen

1 cup fat-free cholesterol-free egg product (from 8-oz. carton) or
    4 eggs, lightly beaten
1/2 cup shredded American cheese (2 oz.)
1/2 teaspoon onion powder
1 tablespoon butter or margarine
1 cup chopped broccoli
1/2 cup shredded carrot
1/4 cup chopped red or green bell pepper
2 tablespoons sliced ripe olives
2 pita breads (6 inch), cut in half to form pockets

1. In medium bowl, mix egg product, cheese and onion powder; set aside.

2. In 10-inch skillet, melt butter over medium heat. Add broccoli, carrot, bell pepper and olives; cook 3 to 5 minutes, stirring frequently, until vegetables are crisp-tender.

3. Pour egg mixture over vegetables; reduce heat to low. Cook, stirring occasionally from outside edge to center, allowing uncooked egg mixture to flow to bottom of skillet, until center is set but still moist.

4. Spoon egg mixture evenly into pita bread halves.

1 Sandwich: Calories 210 (Calories from Fat 80); Total Fat 9g (Saturated Fat 4.5g; Trans Fat 0g); Cholesterol 25mg; Sodium 420mg; Total Carbohydrate 22g (Dietary Fiber 3g; Sugars 3g); Protein 13g
% Daily Value: Vitamin A 80%; Vitamin C 35%; Calcium 15%; Iron 15%
Exchanges: 1 1/2 Starch, 1 Very Lean Meat, 1 1/2 Fat
Carbohydrate Choices: 1 1/2

scrambled egg and veggie pockets

basil-zucchini-potato frittata

start to finish / **25 MINUTES**

4 servings

> "A frittata is almost as quick to make as scrambled eggs and I like to use up leftover vegetables. Eating more vegetables is a family goal we strive for."
>
> *—Kelly*

1 teaspoon olive or canola oil
1/2 medium red bell pepper, chopped (1/2 cup)
1 small onion, chopped (1/3 cup)
1 cup refrigerated shredded hash-brown potatoes (from 20-oz. bag)
1 medium zucchini, shredded (about 2 cups)
1 tablespoon water
3 whole eggs plus 3 egg whites, lightly beaten, or 1 1/4 cups fat-free cholesterol-free egg product (from two 8-oz. cartons)
2 tablespoons chopped fresh basil or 1 teaspoon dried basil leaves
1/2 teaspoon garlic salt
1 cup reduced-fat tomato pasta sauce, heated

1. In 10-inch nonstick skillet, heat oil over medium-high heat. Add bell pepper and onion; cook 5 minutes, stirring frequently.

2. Reduce heat to medium. Add potatoes, zucchini and water; cover and cook 5 to 6 minutes, adding an additional 1 tablespoon water if necessary to prevent sticking, until vegetables are tender.

3. Meanwhile, in medium bowl, mix beaten eggs and egg whites, the basil and garlic salt until well blended.

4. Pour egg mixture over vegetables. Reduce heat to medium-low; cover and cook 7 to 10 minutes, lifting edges occasionally to allow uncooked egg mixture to flow to bottom of skillet, until egg mixture is set but still moist on top. Cut into wedges; serve topped with warm pasta sauce.

1 Serving: Calories 210 (Calories from Fat 70); Total Fat 7g (Saturated Fat 2g; Trans Fat 0g); Cholesterol 160mg; Sodium 530mg; Total Carbohydrate 27g (Dietary Fiber 3g; Sugars 8g); Protein 10g
% Daily Value: Vitamin A 45%; Vitamin C 45%; Calcium 6%; Iron 8%
Exchanges: 1 1/2 Starch, 1 Very Lean Meat, 1 Fat
Carbohydrate Choices: 2

cheesy tomato
frittata

start to finish / **25 MINUTES**

"I like to make this scrumptious frittata for a holiday main dish. I add broccoli or any green vegetable to the skillet before adding the egg mixture and top it with red tomato slices. It just makes it a little more festive."

—Anne

3 whole eggs plus 3 egg whites, lightly beaten, or 1 1/4 cups fat-free cholesterol-free egg product (from two 8-oz. cartons)
1/4 cup fat-free (skim) milk
1/4 teaspoon salt
1/4 teaspoon ground red pepper (cayenne)
1 teaspoon lemon juice
1 teaspoon olive or canola oil
1/4 cup chopped fresh parsley
2 medium roma (plum) tomatoes, thinly sliced
1/2 cup shredded reduced-fat Swiss cheese (2 oz.)
2 tablespoons shredded Parmesan cheese

1. In medium bowl, mix beaten eggs and egg whites, the milk, salt, ground red pepper and lemon juice until well blended.

2. Set oven control to broil. In 8-inch ovenproof nonstick skillet, heat oil over medium-low heat. Pour egg mixture into skillet; sprinkle with parsley. Cover; cook 10 to 15 minutes, lifting edges occasionally to allow uncooked egg mixture to flow to bottom of skillet, until egg mixture is set but still moist on top. Arrange tomatoes over egg mixture.

3. Broil 6 to 8 inches from heat 1 to 3 minutes. Remove from broiler. Sprinkle both cheeses over top; broil 1 minute longer or until cheeses are melted. Cut into wedges to serve.

1 Serving: Calories 130 (Calories from Fat 60); Total Fat 7g (Saturated Fat 2.5g; Trans Fat 0g); Cholesterol 165mg; Sodium 510mg; Total Carbohydrate 4g (Dietary Fiber 0g; Sugars 3g); Protein 13g
% Daily Value: Vitamin A 20%; Vitamin C 8%; Calcium 20%; Iron 6%
Exchanges: 2 Lean Meat, 1/2 Fat
Carbohydrate Choices: 0

cheesy potato and sausage
frittata

start to finish **/ 35 MINUTES**

4 servings

6 oz. bulk light turkey and pork sausage

4 cups frozen potatoes O'Brien with onions and peppers (from 28-oz. bag)

1 cup fat-free cholesterol-free egg product (from 8-oz. carton) or 4 eggs, lightly beaten

1/4 cup fat-free (skim) milk

1/8 teaspoon ground red pepper (cayenne)

1/8 teaspoon pepper

1/8 teaspoon fennel seed, crushed, if desired

1/2 cup finely shredded reduced-fat Cheddar cheese (2 oz.)

1. Heat 12-inch nonstick skillet over high heat. Add sausage; cook 4 to 5 minutes, stirring frequently, until no longer pink. Remove sausage from skillet; drain on paper towels. Return sausage to skillet. Gently stir in potatoes.

2. In small bowl, mix egg product and remaining ingredients except cheese until well blended. Pour egg mixture evenly over potato mixture; cover and cook over medium-low heat 10 minutes.

3. Uncover; cook 5 to 8 minutes longer or until egg product mixture is set but still moist on top. Remove from heat. Sprinkle cheese over top. Let stand until cheese is melted, 3 to 5 minutes. Cut into wedges to serve.

1 Serving: Calories 300 (Calories from Fat 80); Total Fat 9g (Saturated Fat 3.5g; Trans Fat 0g); Cholesterol 35mg; Sodium 710mg; Total Carbohydrate 36g (Dietary Fiber 4g; Sugars 3g); Protein 21g
% Daily Value: Vitamin A 10%; Vitamin C 20%; Calcium 15%; Iron 15%
Exchanges: 2 1/2 Starch, 2 Lean Meat
Carbohydrate Choices: 2 1/2

cheesy potato and sausage frittata

hickory ham and potato frittata

4 servings

> *"I look for recipes that have milk in them because my son doesn't like to drink milk. This way, I can feel good about what I am serving, I know he is getting the vitamins he needs and the kids love it!"*
>
> *—Lori*

3/4 cup finely chopped 97%-fat-free hickory-smoked ham (about 4 oz.)

2 cups chopped red potatoes (3/4 lb.)

2 medium onions, chopped (1 cup)

1/2 medium green bell pepper, chopped (1/2 cup)

3/4 cup fat-free (skim) milk

3 whole eggs plus 3 egg whites, lightly beaten, or 1 1/4 cups fat-free cholesterol-free egg product (from two 8-oz. cartons)

1/4 teaspoon salt

1/4 teaspoon pepper

1/2 cup shredded reduced-fat sharp Cheddar cheese (2 oz.)

1. Heat 10-inch nonstick skillet over high heat. Reduce heat to medium-high. Add ham; cook 2 to 3 minutes, stirring frequently, until lightly browned. Remove ham from skillet; cover to keep warm.

2. To same skillet, place potatoes, onions, bell pepper and 1/2 cup of the milk. Heat to boiling. Reduce heat to medium; cover tightly and simmer 5 to 6 minutes or just until potatoes are tender.

3. Meanwhile, in small bowl, mix eggs and egg whites, the remaining 1/4 cup milk, the salt and pepper until well blended. Stir ham and egg mixture into potato mixture. Reduce heat to medium-low; cover and cook without stirring for 10 minutes.

4. Remove skillet from heat; remove cover (eggs will not appear completely cooked). Sprinkle cheese over top. Let stand 2 to 3 minutes or until egg mixture is set and cheese is melted. Cut into wedges to serve.

1 Serving: Calories 220 (Calories from Fat 60); Total Fat 7g (Saturated Fat 2.5g; Trans Fat 0g); Cholesterol 180mg; Sodium 740mg; Total Carbohydrate 22g (Dietary Fiber 3g; Sugars 7g); Protein 20g
% Daily Value: Vitamin A 10%; Vitamin C 25%; Calcium 20%; Iron 15%
Exchanges: 1 Starch, 1 Vegetable, 2 Lean Meat
Carbohydrate Choices: 1 1/2

easy weeknight entertaining

Haven't yet decided what to take to your during-the-week potluck party? Don't sweat it, just whip up any one (or two) of these quick appetizers—cover or wrap and take with you; they are easily totable.

microwave mexican olé

Prep: 15 min

1 cup fat-free refried beans (from 16-oz. can)
5 to 6 medium green onions, finely chopped (1/3 cup)
1 teaspoon chili powder
1/8 teaspoon each salt, garlic powder, ground cumin
1/2 cup each shredded Cheddar cheese, chopped tomatoes, shredded lettuce
6 cups baked tortilla chips (about 4.5 oz.)

1 In small bowl, mix refried beans, onions, chili powder, salt, garlic powder and cumin. In 9-inch microwavable pie pan, spread mixture evenly.

2 Microwave on High 1 1/2 to 2 1/2 minutes or until thoroughly heated. Sprinkle with cheese. Microwave on High 1 minute longer or until cheese is melted.

3 Sprinkle tomatoes and lettuce over top. Serve immediately with chips.

6 servings

fresh strawberry fruit dip

Prep: 10 min; Chill: 1 hr

1 container (6 oz.) vanilla custard-style low-fat yogurt
1 container (8 oz.) reduced-fat or fat-free cream cheese
2 tablespoons sugar
1 cup sliced fresh strawberries
1/2 teaspoon vanilla

1 In blender or food processor, process yogurt, cream cheese and sugar until smooth. Add strawberries and vanilla; process about 1 minute or until smooth. Chill 1 hour to blend flavors.

2 Serve with cut-up pineapple or banana chunks, strawberries and apple wedges.

18 servings (2 tablespoons each)

bacon-tater snacks

Prep: 20 min

3 slices lean turkey bacon
10 small new red potatoes, unpeeled, halved
1/2 cup reduced-fat sour cream
2 medium green onions, sliced (2 tablespoons)
1/2 teaspoon dried dill weed
1/4 cup grated Parmesan cheese

1 Cook bacon as directed on package. Cool slightly. Crumble; set aside.

2 In 12 x 8-inch (2-quart) microwavable dish, place potatoes, cut side down. Add 2 tablespoons water. Cover tightly with microwavable plastic wrap.

3 Microwave on High 9 to 12 minutes, rotating dish 1/4 turn halfway through cooking, until tender. Let stand 3 minutes. Drain; cool 5 minutes.

4 Meanwhile, in small bowl, mix sour cream, onions and dill.

5 Turn potatoes over. If necessary, trim thin slice off rounded bottom of each potato half to make potatoes stand upright. Sprinkle with pepper and Parmesan cheese, sour cream mixture and bacon.

20 snacks

bacon-tater snacks

pasta
frittata

4 servings

"My kids love pasta, and you can use any pasta shape you have on hand in this yummy egg dish. For a quick (and neat) way to cut this omelet into wedges, I use my pizza cutter."

—Sharon

8 oz. uncooked vermicelli, broken in half

1 cup fat-free cholesterol-free egg product (from 8-oz. carton) or 4 eggs, lightly beaten

1/3 cup fat-free (skim) milk

3/4 teaspoon dried oregano leaves

1/8 teaspoon ground red pepper (cayenne)

8 medium green onions, finely chopped (1/2 cup)

1 teaspoon olive or canola oil

3/4 cup shredded reduced-fat sharp Cheddar cheese (3 oz.)

1. Cook vermicelli as directed on package. Drain; rinse with hot water.

2. Meanwhile, in small bowl, mix egg product, milk, 1/2 teaspoon of the salt, the oregano and ground red pepper until well blended. Stir in onions.

3. In 10-inch nonstick skillet, heat oil over medium heat. Spread cooked vermicelli in hot skillet; pour egg product mixture evenly over top. Reduce heat to medium-low; cover and cook 13 to 15 minutes or until center is almost set.

4. Remove skillet from heat. Sprinkle remaining 1/4 teaspoon salt and the cheese over vermicelli mixture. Cover; let stand 2 minutes or until egg mixture is set and cheese is melted. Serve from skillet, or run pancake turner around edge of skillet to loosen and slide out onto serving plate. Cut into wedges. If desired, garnish with additional chopped green onions.

1 Serving: Calories 300 (Calories from Fat 35); Total Fat 4g (Saturated Fat 1.5g; Trans Fat 0g); Cholesterol 0mg; Sodium 550mg; Total Carbohydrate 49g (Dietary Fiber 4g; Sugars 3g); Protein 20g
% Daily Value: Vitamin A 10%; Vitamin C 2%; Calcium 20%; Iron 20%
Exchanges: 2 1/2 Starch, 1/2 Other Carbohydrate, 1 Vegetable, 1 1/2 Very Lean Meat
Carbohydrate Choices: 3

canadian bacon–tomato frittata SUPER EXPRESS

start to finish / **20 MINUTES**

4 servings

"I love serving this pretty frittata, with the extra veggies. I like to use Canadian bacon, because it is very lean and just a little bit of it gives lots of flavor with very little fat."
— Sally

3 eggs, lightly beaten, or 3/4 cup fat-free cholesterol-free egg product (from 8-oz. carton)

3 tablespoons fat-free (skim) milk

1 teaspoon Dijon mustard

1 teaspoon olive or canola oil

2 oz. Canadian bacon, chopped (1/2 cup)

1/4 cup chopped green bell pepper

1/2 medium onion, chopped (1/4 cup)

1 small tomato, thinly sliced

1/3 cup shredded reduced-fat, reduced-sodium Swiss cheese (1.5 oz.)

2 teaspoons chopped fresh parsley

1. In medium bowl, mix eggs, milk and mustard; set aside.

2. In 8-inch nonstick skillet, heat oil over medium heat. Add bacon, bell pepper and onion; cook 4 to 5 minutes, stirring frequently, until bell pepper and onion are crisp-tender.

3. Pour egg mixture over bacon mixture. Cook, lifting edges occasionally to allow uncooked egg mixture to flow to bottom of skillet, until egg mixture is set but still moist on top.

4. Arrange tomato slices over top; sprinkle with cheese. Cover skillet; cook just until cheese is melted and top is set. Sprinkle parsley over top. Cut into wedges to serve.

1 Serving: Calories 120 (Calories from Fat 60); Total Fat 7g (Saturated Fat 2g; Trans Fat 0g); Cholesterol 170mg; Sodium 290mg; Total Carbohydrate 4g (Dietary Fiber 0g; Sugars 3g); Protein 11g
% Daily Value: Vitamin A 10%; Vitamin C 10%; Calcium 15%; Iron 4%
Exchanges: 1 1/2 Very Lean Meat, 1 1/2 Fat
Carbohydrate Choices: 0

spinach-tomato
frittata

start to finish **/ 35 MINUTES**

4 servings

> "I've noticed that my kids eat better when they help prepare meals. I have one tear the spinach while another measures the ingredients in this easy frittata. When it comes to cleanup, it's all hands on deck."
>
> —Cheri

3 whole eggs plus 3 egg whites, lightly beaten, or 1 1/4 cups fat-free cholesterol-free egg product (from two 8-oz. cartons)

1/3 cup grated Parmesan cheese

1/2 teaspoon garlic powder

1/2 teaspoon dried basil leaves

1/4 teaspoon salt

1/4 teaspoon pepper

1/8 teaspoon ground nutmeg

1 teaspoon canola or soybean oil

6 oz. fresh spinach, torn into bite-size pieces (about 6 cups loosely packed)

5 to 6 cherry tomatoes, sliced

1. In small bowl, mix beaten eggs and egg whites, the cheese, garlic powder, basil, salt, pepper and nutmeg; set aside.

2. In 9- or 10-inch nonstick skillet with sloping sides (omelet or crepe pan), heat oil over medium heat. Add spinach; cover and cook 2 to 3 minutes, stirring once or twice and watching carefully to prevent burning, until spinach is slightly wilted (if necessary, add 2 tablespoons water if spinach is well drained).

3. Spread spinach evenly in skillet; top evenly with tomato slices. Pour egg mixture over top. Reduce heat to low; cover and cook 12 to 15 minutes or until egg mixture is set but still moist on top. Cut into wedges to serve.

1 Serving: Calories 130 (Calories from Fat 70); Total Fat 8g (Saturated Fat 3g; Trans Fat 0g); Cholesterol 165mg; Sodium 420mg; Total Carbohydrate 4g (Dietary Fiber 2g; Sugars 2g); Protein 12g
% Daily Value: Vitamin A 90%; Vitamin C 15%; Calcium 20%; Iron 10%
Exchanges: 1 Vegetable, 1 1/2 Medium-Fat Meat
Carbohydrate Choices: 0

southwest chicken
hash browns

start to finish **/ 30 MINUTES**

2 servings

2 boneless, skinless chicken breasts, cut into 1/4- to 1/2-inch pieces
1/2 cup finely chopped red onion
2 large red potatoes, shredded (about 3 1/2 cups)
4 teaspoons chopped fresh cilantro, if desired
1/2 teaspoon salt
1 tablespoon olive or canola oil
1/4 cup fat-free sour cream
1/4 cup chunky-style salsa

1. In medium bowl, mix chicken and onion. Rinse shredded potatoes with cold water; drain on paper towels. Add to chicken mixture. Stir in cilantro, if desired, and salt.

2. In 10-inch nonstick skillet, heat 2 teaspoons of the oil over medium-high heat. Spread potato mixture evenly in skillet. Cook, without stirring, 6 to 9 minutes or until chicken is no longer pink in center and bottom of potato mixture is golden brown and crisp.

3. Place large plate over skillet; invert potato mixture onto plate. Add remaining teaspoon oil to skillet. Slip potato mixture back into skillet, browned side up; cook 5 to 7 minutes, pressing lightly with pancake turner, until golden brown and crisp.

4. With pancake turner, divide chicken mixture in half; place on 2 plates. Top each with sour cream and salsa.

1 Serving: Calories 300 (Calories from Fat 50); Total Fat 6g (Saturated Fat 1g; Trans Fat 0g); Cholesterol 35mg; Sodium 340mg; Total Carbohydrate 48g (Dietary Fiber 5g; Sugars 2g); Protein 18g
% Daily Value: Vitamin A 0%; Vitamin C 15%; Calcium 4%; Iron 8%
Exchanges: 3 Starch, 1 1/2 Very Lean Meat, 1/2 Fat
Carbohydrate Choices: 3

bagel and cheese bake

6 servings

"This low-fat strata uses bagels instead of bread. The turkey bacon and reduced-fat cheese keep the fat and calories low."

—Kathy

1 medium onion, chopped (1/2 cup)

6 slices turkey bacon, cut into small pieces

3 plain bagels (3- to 4-inch)

3/4 cup shredded reduced-fat sharp Cheddar cheese (3 oz.)

3 cups fat-free (skim) milk

1 cup fat-free cholesterol-free egg product (from 8-oz. carton) or 4 eggs, lightly beaten

2 tablespoons chopped fresh parsley or 2 teaspoons dried parsley flakes

1/4 teaspoon pepper

1/3 cup grated Parmesan cheese

1. Spray 13 x 9-inch (3-quart) glass baking dish with cooking spray. In 8-inch nonstick skillet, cook onion and bacon over medium heat 4 to 6 minutes, stirring occasionally, until onion is tender. Meanwhile, slice each bagel horizontally into 4 thin slices.

2. Place 6 bagel slices in bottom of dish; sprinkle with onion mixture and Cheddar cheese. Top with remaining 6 bagel slices.

3. In large bowl, mix milk, egg product, parsley and pepper. Pour egg product mixture over bagels; sprinkle with Parmesan cheese. Let stand at room temperature 15 minutes. Meanwhile, heat oven to 350°F.

4. Bake 35 to 40 minutes or until set and golden brown. Cut into squares to serve.

1 Serving: Calories 240 (Calories from Fat 50); Total Fat 6g (Saturated Fat 2.5g; Trans Fat 0g); Cholesterol 15mg; Sodium 750mg; Total Carbohydrate 27g (Dietary Fiber 2g; Sugars 9g); Protein 20g
% Daily Value: Vitamin A 15%; Vitamin C 4%; Calcium 35%; Iron 15%
Exchanges: 1 1/2 Starch, 1/2 Other Carbohydrate, 2 Lean Meat
Carbohydrate Choices: 2

italian french toast SUPER EXPRESS

start to finish / **20 MINUTES**

4 servings (2 slices french toast each)

3 eggs, lightly beaten, or 3/4 cup fat-free cholesterol-free egg product (from 8-oz. carton)
3/4 cup fat-free (skim) milk
1/4 teaspoon garlic powder
1 teaspoon canola or soybean oil
8 slices light Italian bread
2 teaspoons Italian seasoning
1/2 cup shredded mozzarella cheese (2 oz.)

1. In shallow bowl or pie pan, mix beaten eggs, milk and garlic powder until well blended.

2. Heat 12-inch nonstick skillet or griddle over medium heat or to 375°F. Add oil, tilting skillet to spread oil. Dip each slice of bread into egg mixture, turning to coat both sides. Place in hot skillet; sprinkle each slice with 1/4 teaspoon Italian seasoning.

3. Cook 2 to 3 minutes or until golden brown. Turn bread; sprinkle with cheese. Cook 2 to 3 minutes longer or until bread is golden brown and cheese is melted.

1 Serving: Calories 230 (Calories from Fat 90); Total Fat 9g (Saturated Fat 3.5g; Trans Fat 0g); Cholesterol 170mg; Sodium 380mg; Total Carbohydrate 24g (Dietary Fiber 1g; Sugars 3g); Protein 14g
% Daily Value: Vitamin A 8%; Vitamin C 0%; Calcium 20%; Iron 10%
Exchanges: 1 1/2 Starch, 1 1/2 Medium-Fat Meat
Carbohydrate Choices: 1 1/2

french toast with raspberry-cranberry syrup

4 servings

start to finish / **40 MINUTES**

French Toast

2 whole eggs plus 1 egg white, lightly beaten, or 1/2 cup fat-free cholesterol-free egg product (from 8-oz. carton)

1 cup fat-free (skim) milk

2 teaspoons rum extract

1/4 teaspoon ground nutmeg

8 slices (1 inch thick) French bread

Syrup

1/2 cup frozen (thawed) raspberry blend juice concentrate

1/2 cup jellied cranberry sauce

1 tablespoon powdered sugar

1. Heat oven to 425°F. In medium bowl, mix beaten eggs and egg white, the milk, rum extract and nutmeg until well blended.

2. Dip bread slices into egg mixture, coating both sides well. Place in ungreased 11 x 7-inch (2-quart) glass baking dish. Pour remaining eggnog mixture over bread slices. Let stand at room temperature 15 minutes.

3. Spray cookie sheet with cooking spray. Remove bread slices from dish; place on cookie sheet. Bake 12 to 15 minutes or until golden brown, turning slices once halfway through baking.

4. In 1-quart saucepan, mix syrup ingredients; cook over medium-low heat, stirring occasionally, until cranberry sauce and sugar have melted. Serve French toast with syrup.

1 Serving: Calories 300 (Calories from Fat 40); Total Fat 4.5g (Saturated Fat 1.5g; Trans Fat 0g); Cholesterol 105mg; Sodium 340mg; Total Carbohydrate 55g (Dietary Fiber 2g; Sugars 32g); Protein 10g
% Daily Value: Vitamin A 6%; Vitamin C 6%; Calcium 15%; Iron 10%
Exchanges: 1 1/2 Starch, 2 Other Carbohydrate, 1 Medium-Fat Meat
Carbohydrate Choices: 3 1/2

french toast with raspberry-cranberry syrup

honey wheat
french toast SUPER EXPRESS

start to finish **/ 20 MINUTES**

4 servings (2 slices French toast and 2 tablespoons honey each)

"We've been working at increasing the amount of whole grains we eat. We eat a lot of breads and cereals, and if we just eat whole wheat bread, that is a good start."
—Augusto

3 eggs, lightly beaten, or 3/4 cup fat-free cholesterol-free
    egg product (from 8-oz. carton)
3/4 cup fat-free (skim) milk
1 teaspoon sugar
1/4 teaspoon ground nutmeg
1 teaspoon vanilla
1/2 teaspoon grated orange peel
1 teaspoon canola or soybean oil
8 slices honey wheat bread
1/2 cup honey, heated

1. In shallow bowl or pie pan, mix eggs, milk, sugar, nutmeg, vanilla and orange peel until well blended.

2. Heat 12-inch nonstick skillet or griddle over medium heat or to 375°F. Add oil, tilting skillet to spread oil. Dip each slice of bread into egg mixture, turning to coat both sides. Place in hot skillet; cook 4 to 6 minutes, turning once, until golden brown. Serve with warm honey.

1 Serving: Calories 350 (Calories from Fat 60); Total Fat 7g (Saturated Fat 1.5g; Trans Fat 0g); Cholesterol 160mg; Sodium 340mg; Total Carbohydrate 63g (Dietary Fiber 2g; Sugars 41g); Protein 11g
% Daily Value: Vitamin A 6%; Vitamin C 0%; Calcium 15%; Iron 10%
Exchanges: 2 Starch, 2 Other Carbohydrate, 1 Medium-Fat Meat
Carbohydrate Choices: 4

french toast
strata

start to finish **/ 1 HOUR 15 MINUTES**

8 servings

"Though the recipe calls for strawberries, I will use whatever fresh fruit I have on hand, raspberries, pears or apples— I don't mind making my own substitutions."
—Jeanne

1/2 cup packed light brown sugar

2 tablespoons butter or margarine, melted

8 diagonal slices (1/2 inch thick) soft-crust French bread

4 whole eggs plus 4 egg whites, lightly beaten, or 1 1/2 cups fat-free cholesterol-free egg product (from two 8-oz. cartons)

1 3/4 cups fat-free (skim) milk

1 teaspoon ground ginger

2 cups sliced fresh strawberries

Powdered sugar

1. Spray 11 x 7-inch (2-quart) glass baking dish with cooking spray. In small bowl, mix brown sugar and butter until well blended. Spread mixture in bottom of dish. Arrange bread slices over brown sugar mixture.

2. In medium bowl, mix beaten eggs and egg whites, the milk and ginger until well blended. Pour over bread in dish. Let stand at room temperature 15 minutes. Meanwhile, heat oven to 350°F.

3. Bake 45 to 50 minutes or until center is puffed and knife inserted in center comes out clean. Immediately cut into squares; serve with strawberries and powdered sugar.

1 Serving: Calories 270 (Calories from Fat 80); Total Fat 9g (Saturated Fat 3.5g; Trans Fat 0g); Cholesterol 155mg; Sodium 280mg; Total Carbohydrate 38g (Dietary Fiber 2g; Sugars 26g); Protein 11g
% Daily Value: Vitamin A 10%; Vitamin C 25%; Calcium 15%; Iron 10%
Exchanges: 1 Starch, 1 1/2 Other Carbohydrate, 1 Very Lean Meat, 1 1/2 Fat
Carbohydrate Choices: 2 1/2

20-minute meals

chapter 2

"Recipes in 20

minutes—it's

exactly what I'm

looking for—it fits

with our

schedule."

—Libby P.

SUPER EXPRESS *Ready in 20 minutes or less*

navajo
taco salad SUPER EXPRESS

start to finish / **20 MINUTES**

4 servings

1 medium green bell pepper, coarsely chopped (1 cup)
1 medium onion, coarsely chopped (1/2 cup)
1 can (15 oz.) kidney beans, drained
1 cup chunky-style salsa
1/2 cup frozen whole kernel corn (from 1-lb. bag)
4 oz. baked tortilla chips (about 5 1/2 cups)
6 cups torn romaine
1 cup shredded Cheddar cheese (4 oz.)
1/4 cup fat-free sour cream
Fresh cilantro leaves, if desired

1. Heat 10-inch nonstick skillet over medium-high heat. Add bell pepper and onion; cook 5 minutes, stirring frequently, until almost tender. Stir in kidney beans, salsa and corn. Cover; simmer 3 minutes, stirring occasionally, until vegetables are tender and mixture is hot.

2. Meanwhile, arrange chips on individual dinner plates. Top each with romaine. Spoon vegetable-bean mixture over lettuce. Sprinkle each with cheese. Top with sour cream and cilantro, if desired.

1 Serving: Calories 420 (Calories from Fat 100); Total Fat 11g (Saturated Fat 6g; Trans Fat 0g); Cholesterol 30mg; Sodium 710mg; Total Carbohydrate 64g (Dietary Fiber 12g; Sugars 8g); Protein 22g
% Daily Value: Vitamin A 70%; Vitamin C 60%; Calcium 25%; Iron 35%
Exchanges: 4 Starch, 1 1/2 Medium-Fat Meat
Carbohydrate Choices: 3 1/2

40   *pillsbury good for you!*

mandarin–smoked
turkey salad SUPER EXPRESS

start to finish **/ 15 MINUTES**

6 servings (1 1/2 cups each)

> *"If there is an ingredient I don't have on hand or that my kids don't like, I'll just use something else. I might use green cabbage or bagged coleslaw mix in this salad."*
>
> *—Neil*

Dressing
1/2 cup orange marmalade
2 tablespoons soy sauce
4 teaspoons cider vinegar
1/8 teaspoon ginger

Salad
4 cups shredded Chinese (napa) cabbage
2 cups shredded iceberg lettuce
2 1/2 cups cubed smoked turkey (about 3/4 lb.)
1 cup fresh pea pods, trimmed, cut diagonally into 1-inch pieces
1 can (15 oz.) mandarin orange segments, drained

1. In 1-quart saucepan, mix dressing ingredients until well blended. Heat over medium heat, stirring frequently, until marmalade is melted. Cool 5 minutes.

2. Meanwhile, in large bowl, toss cabbage, lettuce, turkey and pea pods.

3. Gently stir orange segments into salad. Pour dressing over salad; toss gently to coat. Serve immediately.

1 Serving: Calories 210 (Calories from Fat 25); Total Fat 3g (Saturated Fat 1g; Trans Fat 0g); Cholesterol 50mg; Sodium 390mg; Total Carbohydrate 27g (Dietary Fiber 2g; Sugars 20g); Protein 20g
% Daily Value: Vitamin A 50%; Vitamin C 90%; Calcium 8%; Iron 10%
Exchanges: 1/2 Starch, 1 Other Carbohydrate, 1 Vegetable, 2 1/2 Very Lean Meat
Carbohydrate Choices: 2

warm italian
shrimp salad SUPER EXPRESS

start to finish **/ 15 MINUTES**

4 servings (1 3/4 cups each)

"I'm trying to get my family used to whole wheat pasta, so I use half whole wheat and half regular rotini for us to gradually get used to it."

—Cheri

3 cups uncooked rotini pasta (8 oz.)

1/2 lb. cooked peeled deveined medium shrimp, thawed if frozen, tail shells removed

2 large tomatoes or 6 roma (plum) tomatoes, chopped (about 2 cups)

1/4 cup chopped fresh basil

1/4 cup shredded Parmesan cheese (1 oz.)

2 tablespoons chopped ripe olives

1/4 teaspoon garlic powder

1/8 teaspoon salt

Dash pepper

3 tablespoons red wine vinegar

2 tablespoons olive or canola oil

1. Cook pasta as directed on package. Place shrimp in colander or strainer; rinse briefly with cold water. Let stand in colander until pasta is cooked. To drain pasta, pour over shrimp in colander.

2. Meanwhile, in large bowl, mix remaining ingredients.

3. Gently stir cooked pasta and shrimp into tomato mixture. Serve immediately.

1 Serving: Calories 380 (Calories from Fat 100); Total Fat 11g (Saturated Fat 2.5g; Trans Fat 0g); Cholesterol 115mg; Sodium 580mg; Total Carbohydrate 50g (Dietary Fiber 5g; Sugars 3g); Protein 23g
% Daily Value: Vitamin A 20%; Vitamin C 30%; Calcium 15%; Iron 25%
Exchanges: 3 Starch, 1 Vegetable, 1 1/2 Very Lean Meat, 1 1/2 Fat
Carbohydrate Choices: 3

warm italian shrimp salad

california
chicken salad

start to finish / **15 MINUTES**

10 servings (1 2/3 cups each)

"I love the taste of bacon, but am careful not to use too much. By reading labels, I've discovered that Canadian bacon contains fewer calories than regular bacon and still has great flavor, so I can feel good about using it my recipes."

—Andi

Salad

3 1/2 cups torn leaf lettuce

3 1/2 cups torn romaine

3 boneless, skinless chicken breasts (3/4 lb.), cooked, cut into bite-size pieces

2 oz. Canadian bacon, sliced, cut into thin strips (1 cup)

6 medium green onions, sliced (6 tablespoons)

1 medium tomato, chopped (3/4 cup)

Vinaigrette

1/4 cup balsamic vinegar

2 tablespoons canola or soybean oil

1 teaspoon Dijon mustard

1 clove garlic, minced

1. In large bowl, mix salad ingredients.

2. In small bowl, mix vinaigrette ingredients until well blended. Just before serving, pour vinaigrette over salad; toss gently.

1 Serving: Calories 190 (Calories from Fat 100); Total Fat 11g (Saturated Fat 1.5g; Trans Fat 0g); Cholesterol 50mg; Sodium 250mg; Total Carbohydrate 5g (Dietary Fiber 2g; Sugars 3g); Protein 19g
% Daily Value: Vitamin A 25%; Vitamin C 30%; Calcium 4%; Iron 8%
Exchanges: 1 Vegetable, 2 1/2 Very Lean Meat, 2 Fat
Carbohydrate Choices: 1/2

layered
santa fe salad SUPER EXPRESS

start to finish / **10 MINUTES**

4 servings

> *"I try to get my kids to help out wherever they can. This is one they can easily help with—they can help layer, open cans and packages, and toss the finished salad."*
>
> —Lisa

3/4 cup chunky-style salsa

1 teaspoon sugar

3 teaspoons chili powder

1 bag (10 oz.) mixed salad greens (8 cups loosely packed)

1 cup diced cooked chicken

1 container (8 oz.) fat-free sour cream

1 cup shredded reduced-fat Cheddar cheese (4 oz.)

2 tablespoons sliced ripe olives (from 3.8 oz. can), drained

1 cup broken baked tortilla chips

1. In small bowl, mix salsa, sugar and chili powder.

2. In 13 x 9-inch (3-quart) glass baking dish, arrange salad greens. Top with chicken. Spoon salsa mixture evenly over chicken. Top with spoonfuls of sour cream. Sprinkle with cheese, olives and chips. Serve immediately.

1 Serving: Calories 250 (Calories from Fat 50); Total Fat 6g (Saturated Fat 2g; Trans Fat 0g); Cholesterol 40mg; Sodium 780mg; Total Carbohydrate 30g (Dietary Fiber 4g; Sugars 6g); Protein 22g
% Daily Value: Vitamin A 70%; Vitamin C 35%; Calcium 35%; Iron 15%
Exchanges: 2 Starch, 2 Lean Meat
Carbohydrate Choices: 2

fast fajita and
vegetable pita *SUPER EXPRESS*

start to finish **/ 10 MINUTES**

6 sandwiches

1/4 cup Italian dressing

2 to 3 teaspoons lime juice

1/2 lb. thinly sliced, cooked roast beef, cut into strips (2 cups)

1/2 cup chopped fresh broccoli

1 small tomato, chopped (1/2 cup)

3 pita breads (6 inch), cut in half to form pockets

6 leaves lettuce

1. In medium bowl, mix dressing and lime juice. Add roast beef, broccoli and tomato; toss to coat.

2. To serve, line pita bread halves with lettuce. Fill each with about 1/2 cup beef mixture. If desired, drizzle with additional Italian dressing.

1 Sandwich: Calories 240 (Calories from Fat 100); Total Fat 11g (Saturated Fat 3g; Trans Fat 0g); Cholesterol 35mg; Sodium 280mg; Total Carbohydrate 19g (Dietary Fiber 1g; Sugars 2g); Protein 15g
% Daily Value: Vitamin A 6%; Vitamin C 8%; Calcium 4%; Iron 15%
Exchanges: 1 Starch, 1 1/2 Lean Meat, 1 1/2 Fat
Carbohydrate Choices: 1

mushroom-ham
toast toppers SUPER EXPRESS

6 servings

2 cups fat-free (skim) milk
3 tablespoons cornstarch
1/4 teaspoon salt
1/4 teaspoon dried dill weed
1 teaspoon Dijon mustard
1 teaspoon butter or margarine
1 package (8 oz.) sliced fresh mushrooms (3 cups)
6 slices rye bread
1 package (6 oz.) thinly sliced cooked ham

1. In medium bowl, mix milk, cornstarch, salt, dill and mustard until smooth; set aside.

2. In 8-inch nonstick skillet, melt butter over medium-high heat. Add mushrooms; cook about 2 minutes, stirring occasionally.

3. Reduce heat to medium. Gradually add cornstarch mixture, cooking and stirring until bubbly and thickened. Remove from heat; cover to keep warm.

4. Set oven control to broil. Top slices of bread evenly with ham; place on ungreased cookie sheet. Broil 4 to 6 inches from heat 2 to 3 minutes or until thoroughly heated. Serve mushroom mixture over ham-topped rye bread.

1 Serving: Calories 170 (Calories from Fat 40); Total Fat 4.5g (Saturated Fat 1.5g; Trans Fat 0g); Cholesterol 20mg; Sodium 760mg; Total Carbohydrate 22g (Dietary Fiber 2g; Sugars 5g); Protein 12g
% Daily Value: Vitamin A 4%; Vitamin C 0%; Calcium 10%; Iron 8%
Exchanges: 1 1/2 Starch, 1 Very Lean Meat, 1/2 Fat
Carbohydrate Choices: 1 1/2

barbecued
pork fajitas SUPER EXPRESS

start to finish / 20 MINUTES

4 fajitas

"If I have pork loin on hand, I slice it and use it in place of the chops—super-easy!"
—Pam

1 teaspoon ground cumin
1/2 teaspoon garlic-pepper blend
1 lb. boneless pork loin chops, cut into thin bite-size strips
1/2 medium red bell pepper, cut into thin bite-size strips
1/2 medium green bell pepper, cut into thin bite-size strips
1/2 cup red onion slices or 1 medium onion, sliced
1/3 cup barbecue sauce
4 fat-free flour tortillas (8 to 10 inch)

1. In resealable plastic food-storage bag, place cumin and garlic-pepper blend. Seal bag; shake to blend. Add pork; seal bag and shake to coat.

2. Heat 10-inch nonstick skillet over medium-high heat. Add pork; cook and stir 2 minutes.

3. Add bell peppers and onion; cook 2 to 3 minutes, stirring frequently, until pork is no longer pink in center and vegetables are crisp-tender. Stir in barbecue sauce; cook and stir until thoroughly heated. Serve pork mixture in tortillas.

1 Fajita: Calories 380 (Calories from Fat 80); Total Fat 9g (Saturated Fat 3g; Trans Fat 0g); Cholesterol 70mg; Sodium 710mg; Total Carbohydrate 44g (Dietary Fiber 4g; Sugars 7g); Protein 31g
% Daily Value: Vitamin A 20%; Vitamin C 35%; Calcium 8%; Iron 20%
Exchanges: 2 1/2 Starch, 1 Vegetable, 3 Lean Meat
Carbohydrate Choices: 3

tuna salad
sandwiches *SUPER EXPRESS*

start to finish / **15 MINUTES**

4 sandwiches

2 tablespoons fat-free plain yogurt

2 tablespoons reduced-fat mayonnaise or salad dressing

1 can (8 oz.) pineapple tidbits in juice, drained

1 can (6 oz.) white tuna in water, drained, flaked

1/4 cup finely chopped green bell pepper

1/4 cup coarsely chopped water chestnuts

1/2 teaspoon lemon-pepper seasoning

2 tablespoons sunflower nuts

4 kaiser rolls, split

1. In medium bowl, mix yogurt and mayonnaise until well blended. Stir in remaining ingredients except rolls.

2. Fill each roll with about 1/2 cup tuna mixture. Wrap each sandwich securely with foil or plastic wrap; take with you for an on-the-go dinner.

1 Sandwich: Calories 280 (Calories from Fat 70); Total Fat 7g (Saturated Fat 1g; Trans Fat 0.5g); Cholesterol 15mg; Sodium 500mg; Total Carbohydrate 38g (Dietary Fiber 3g; Sugars 9g); Protein 17g
% Daily Value: Vitamin A 0%; Vitamin C 25%; Calcium 8%; Iron 15%
Exchanges: 2 Starch, 1/2 Other Carbohydrate, 1 1/2 Very Lean Meat, 1 Fat
Carbohydrate Choices: 2 1/2

spicy chinese
chicken tacos SUPER EXPRESS

start to finish **/ 20 MINUTES**

6 servings (2 tacos each)

"To make this quick recipe even quicker, I cut up the chicken and veggies the evening before or the morning of our dinner. Then I cover tightly and refrigerate them."
—Renae

1 box (4.6 oz.) taco shells (12 shells)
3 boneless, skinless chicken breasts (3/4 lb.), cut into thin bite-size strips
1 teaspoon grated gingerroot
1 small clove garlic, minced
2 tablespoons soy sauce
1 tablespoon honey
1 large green onion, sliced
1/2 teaspoon crushed red pepper
1 1/2 cups shredded iceberg lettuce

1. If desired, heat taco shells as directed on box.

2. Heat large nonstick skillet over medium-high heat. Add chicken, gingerroot and garlic; cook 3 to 5 minutes, stirring frequently, until lightly browned.

3. Stir in soy sauce, honey, onion and red pepper to coat. Reduce heat to low; cover and cook 5 minutes, stirring occasionally, until chicken is no longer pink in center.

4. To serve, place scant 1/4 cup chicken mixture in each taco shell. Top each with lettuce. Serve immediately.

1 Serving: Calories 180 (Calories from Fat 60); Total Fat 7g (Saturated Fat 1g; Trans Fat 1.5g); Cholesterol 35mg; Sodium 260mg; Total Carbohydrate 18g (Dietary Fiber 2g; Sugars 4g); Protein 14g
% Daily Value: Vitamin A 4%; Vitamin C 0%; Calcium 4%; Iron 6%
Exchanges: 1 Starch, 1 1/2 Very Lean Meat, 1 Fat
Carbohydrate Choices: 1

spicy chinese chicken tacos

olé
beef patties

start to finish **/ 20 MINUTES**

4 servings

"These patties have a little kick to them. I love using only a few ingredients that I already have on hand to get great flavor."
—Phyllis

1/2 lb. extra-lean (at least 90%) ground beef
1/2 lb. lean ground turkey
1/4 cup ketchup
1 teaspoon dried minced onion
1 tablespoon chopped green chiles (from 4.5-oz. can)
1 teaspoon chili powder
Salsa, if desired

1. Set oven control to broil. In large bowl, mix ground beef and turkey. Stir in remaining ingredients. Shape mixture firmly into 4 patties, 1/2 inch thick. Place on broiler pan.

2. Broil 3 to 4 inches from heat 10 to 12 minutes, turning once and watching carefully to prevent burning, until thermometer inserted in center of patties reads 165°F. If desired, serve with salsa.

1 Serving: Calories 180 (Calories from Fat 70); Total Fat 8g (Saturated Fat 2.5g; Trans Fat 0g); Cholesterol 75mg; Sodium 280mg; Total Carbohydrate 5g (Dietary Fiber 0g; Sugars 4g); Protein 24g
% Daily Value: Vitamin A 10%; Vitamin C 2%; Calcium 0%; Iron 10%
Exchanges: 3 1/2 Lean Meat
Carbohydrate Choices: 0

speedy
tortilla soup

start to finish **/ 20 MINUTES**

4 servings (1 1/4 cups each)

"I am always looking for little ways to cut calories and fat. I use low-fat baked tortilla chips in place of traditional fried corn tortilla strips."

—Anne

2 cans (14.5 oz. each) low-sodium chicken broth
4 medium tomatoes, chopped (2 cups)
1/4 cup chopped green chiles (from 4.5-oz. can)
16 baked tortilla chips
1 cup shredded reduced-fat Cheddar-Monterey Jack cheese blend (4 oz.)
Fresh cilantro leaves, if desired

1. In 2-quart saucepan, heat broth to boiling over high heat. Stir in tomatoes and chiles. Return to boiling. Reduce heat to medium-low; cover and simmer 6 to 8 minutes.

2. For each serving, place 4 tortilla chips in individual soup bowl. Top each with 1/4 cup cheese and hot broth mixture. If desired, garnish with fresh cilantro.

1 Serving: Calories 160 (Calories from Fat 70); Total Fat 8g (Saturated Fat 4.5g; Trans Fat 0g); Cholesterol 20mg; Sodium 490mg; Total Carbohydrate 12g (Dietary Fiber 2g; Sugars 2g); Protein 12g
% Daily Value: Vitamin A 20%; Vitamin C 15%; Calcium 20%; Iron 8%
Exchanges: 1/2 Starch, 1 Vegetable, 1 Medium-Fat Meat, 1/2 Fat
Carbohydrate Choices: 1

chicken-tortellini soup SUPER EXPRESS

start to finish **/ 20 MINUTES**

4 servings (2 cups each)

2 cans (14 oz. each) fat-free chicken broth with 1/3 less sodium

3 cups water

5 to 6 medium green onions, sliced (1/3 cup)

1/2 teaspoon dried basil leaves

2 cloves garlic, minced

1/2 lb. precut chicken breast chunks or 2 boneless, skinless chicken breasts (1/2 lb.), cut into 1/2-inch pieces

1 package (9 oz.) refrigerated cheese-filled tortellini

1 cup chopped fresh spinach

1 cup frozen sweet peas (from 1-lb. bag)

1. In 3-quart saucepan or Dutch oven, mix broth, water, onions, basil and garlic. Heat to boiling. Stir in chicken and tortellini. Reduce heat to medium; simmer uncovered 4 minutes.

2. Add spinach and peas; cook 5 minutes, stirring occasionally, until spinach is wilted, tortellini is tender and chicken is no longer pink in center. If desired, season to taste with pepper.

1 Serving: Calories 190 (Calories from Fat 50); Total Fat 6g (Saturated Fat 2.5g; Trans Fat 0g); Cholesterol 90mg; Sodium 500mg; Total Carbohydrate 17g (Dietary Fiber 2g; Sugars 3g); Protein 19g
% Daily Value: Vitamin A 20%; Vitamin C 6%; Calcium 8%; Iron 10%
Exchanges: 1 Starch, 2 1/2 Very Lean Meat, 1 Fat
Carbohydrate Choices: 1

chicken-tortellini soup

rush-hour chili SUPER EXPRESS

start to finish / **20 MINUTES**

4 servings (1 1/4 cups each)

"I try to save myself time and not make the same dinner over and over. I'd serve this quick chili over cooked spaghetti or macaroni, then top with shredded reduced-fat cheese and sour cream."

—Alex

3/4 lb. extra-lean (at least 90%) ground beef
1 can (15.5 or 15 oz.) kidney beans, drained, rinsed
1 can (14.5 oz.) diced tomatoes, undrained
1 can (6 oz.) tomato paste
2 cups cold water
2 teaspoons chili powder

1. In 3-quart nonstick saucepan or Dutch oven, cook ground beef over medium-high heat, stirring frequently, until brown; drain.

2. Stir in remaining ingredients. Heat to boiling. Reduce heat to medium-low; cover and simmer 5 to 7 minutes, stirring occasionally, until thoroughly heated.

1 Serving: Calories 300 (Calories from Fat 70); Total Fat 8g (Saturated Fat 3g; Trans Fat 0g); Cholesterol 55mg; Sodium 540mg; Total Carbohydrate 34g (Dietary Fiber 9g; Sugars 4g); Protein 27g
% Daily Value: Vitamin A 35%; Vitamin C 30%; Calcium 8%; Iron 35%
Exchanges: 2 Starch, 3 Lean Meat
Carbohydrate Choices: 1 1/2

turkey and twists in
tomato-cream
sauce

start to finish / **30 MINUTES**

4 servings (1 3/4 cups each)

3 cups uncooked rotini pasta (8 oz.)
1/3 lb. fully cooked, honey-roasted turkey breast
1 container (15 oz.) refrigerated marinara sauce
1/2 cup reduced-fat sour cream
2 tablespoons finely shredded Parmesan cheese
2 tablespoons chopped fresh parsley

1. In 3-quart saucepan, cook pasta as directed on package, omitting salt. Drain; cover to keep warm.

2. Meanwhile, cut turkey into 1 x 1/4 x 1/4-inch strips. In 8-inch skillet, heat marinara sauce over medium heat. Stir in sour cream until well blended. Stir in turkey; cook until thoroughly heated.

3. Serve cooked sauce over pasta. Sprinkle with cheese and parsley.

---

1 Serving: Calories 430 (Calories from Fat 70); Total Fat 8g (Saturated Fat 2.5g; Trans Fat 0g); Cholesterol 45mg; Sodium 860mg; Total Carbohydrate 68g (Dietary Fiber 5g; Sugars 13g); Protein 24g
% Daily Value: Vitamin A 20%; Vitamin C 15%; Calcium 10%; Iron 20%
Exchanges: 3 1/2 Starch, 1 Other Carbohydrate, 2 Lean Meat
Carbohydrate Choices: 4

tex-mex
pasta *SUPER EXPRESS*

4 servings (1 3/4 cups each)

> "I would use
> whatever beans
> I have on hand
> in this quick
> saucepan
> casserole, like
> great northern or
> kidney. We often
> eat beans,
> because we know
> they are high in
> fiber."
>
> —Todd

1 cup uncooked small pasta shells (7 oz.)
2 cans (14.5 oz. each) whole tomatoes, undrained, cut up
1 can (15 oz.) black beans, drained, rinsed
1 can (4.5 oz.) chopped green chiles
1 cup frozen whole kernel corn (from 1-lb. bag)
1 teaspoon Southwest or Mexican seasoning
Shredded reduced-fat Monterey Jack cheese, if desired

1. Cook pasta as directed on package, omitting salt. Drain; cover to keep warm.

2. Meanwhile, in 2-quart saucepan, mix remaining ingredients. Heat to boiling over medium heat, stirring occasionally. Reduce heat to low; simmer uncovered 10 minutes.

3. Gently stir in cooked pasta. If desired, top individual servings with shredded reduced-fat Monterey Jack cheese.

1 Serving: Calories 380 (Calories from Fat 15); Total Fat 2g (Saturated Fat 0g; Trans Fat 0g); Cholesterol 0mg; Sodium 740mg; Total Carbohydrate 81g (Dietary Fiber 12g; Sugars 9g); Protein 18g
% Daily Value: Vitamin A 15%; Vitamin C 30%; Calcium 15%; Iron 30%
Exchanges: 4 Starch, 1/2 Other Carbohydrate, 2 Vegetable
Carbohydrate Choices: 4 1/2

mushroom and herb
risotto SUPER EXPRESS

start to finish **/ 20 MINUTES**

3 servings (1 1/3 cups each)

1 teaspoon butter or margarine
1 package (8 oz.) sliced fresh mushrooms (3 cups)
1 can (14 oz.) low-sodium chicken broth
1 3/4 cups uncooked instant rice
1 container (5 oz.) reduced-fat garlic-and-herb spreadable cheese
3 tablespoons chopped fresh chives

1. In 10-inch skillet, melt butter over medium heat. Add mushrooms; cook and stir until mushrooms are tender.

2. Add broth; heat to boiling. Remove from heat. Stir in rice. Cover; let stand 5 minutes.

3. Stir in cheese and chives. Return skillet to medium heat; cook and stir until thoroughly heated.

---

1 Serving: Calories 420 (Calories from Fat 120); Total Fat 13g (Saturated Fat 8g; Trans Fat 0.5g); Cholesterol 45mg; Sodium 340mg; Total Carbohydrate 61g (Dietary Fiber 2g; Sugars 3g); Protein 17g
% Daily Value: Vitamin A 8%; Vitamin C 2%; Calcium 25%; Iron 20%
Exchanges: 3 1/2 Starch, 1 Vegetable, 1/2 High-Fat Meat, 1 1/2 Fat
Carbohydrate Choices: 4

beef with mushrooms and noodles SUPER EXPRESS

start to finish **/ 20 MINUTES**

4 servings (1 1/4 cups each)

"I can save even more time by using canned mushrooms instead of the presliced fresh ones."

—Jason

3 1/2 cups uncooked medium egg noodles (6 oz.)
1/2 lb. boneless beef sirloin steak, cut into thin bite-size strips
1/4 teaspoon peppered seasoned salt
1 can (15 oz.) Italian-style tomato sauce
1 package (8 oz.) sliced fresh mushrooms (3 cups)
6 small green onions, cut into 1/2-inch pieces

1. Cook and drain noodles as directed on package, omitting salt. Place on serving platter or in serving bowl; cover to keep warm.

2. Meanwhile, sprinkle beef with seasoned salt. Heat 10-inch nonstick skillet over medium-high heat. Add beef; cook and stir 2 minutes or until brown.

3. Stir in tomato sauce, mushrooms and onions (if necessary, break up larger pieces of tomatoes with spoon). Heat to boiling. Reduce heat to low; simmer uncovered 3 to 5 minutes, stirring occasionally, until vegetables are tender. Pour beef mixture over noodles; toss gently to mix.

1 Serving: Calories 340 (Calories from Fat 70); Total Fat 7g (Saturated Fat 1.5g; Trans Fat 0g); Cholesterol 65mg; Sodium 640mg; Total Carbohydrate 50g (Dietary Fiber 4g; Sugars 9g); Protein 20g
% Daily Value: Vitamin A 15%; Vitamin C 15%; Calcium 4%; Iron 25%
Exchanges: 3 Starch, 1 Vegetable, 1 Lean Meat, 1/2 Fat
Carbohydrate Choices: 3

tuna spaghetti with cheese sauce SUPER EXPRESS

start to finish / **20 MINUTES**

4 servings (1 1/2 cups each)

"This is a great easy recipe and my kids love it. When I cook pasta, I cook extra and keep it on hand for quick dishes like this one."

—Cheri

7 oz. uncooked spaghetti

1 1/2 cups frozen sweet peas (from 1-lb. bag)

1 cup evaporated low-fat milk

1/2 cup reduced-fat process cheese sauce (from a jar)

1/4 teaspoon pepper

2 cans (6 oz. each) tuna in water, drained, flaked

Grated Parmesan cheese, if desired

1. In Dutch oven, cook spaghetti as directed on package, omiting salt, adding peas during last 2 minutes of cooking. Drain in colander; cover to keep warm.

2. In same Dutch oven, mix milk, cheese product and pepper. Cook over medium heat, stirring frequently, until cheese is melted.

3. Gently stir in cooked spaghetti and tuna. Cook over medium heat, stirring occasionally, until thoroughly heated. If desired, sprinkle with grated Parmesan cheese.

1 Serving: Calories 460 (Calories from Fat 100); Total Fat 11g (Saturated Fat 6g; Trans Fat 0g); Cholesterol 60mg; Sodium 910mg; Total Carbohydrate 56g (Dietary Fiber 5g; Sugars 13g); Protein 38g
% Daily Value: Vitamin A 15%; Vitamin C 4%; Calcium 30%; Iron 25%
Exchanges: 3 Starch, 1/2 Other Carbohydrate, 4 Lean Meat
Carbohydrate Choices: 3 1/2

tomato-basil linguine
with chicken SUPER EXPRESS

start to finish / **15 MINUTES**

4 servings (1 1/2 cups each)

"I like to use convenience items like chopped garlic in a jar—it's a handy substitute for fresh. Not only does it save me time, it seems to keep forever in my refrigerator."
—Jessica

5 oz. refrigerated linguine

4 boneless, skinless chicken breasts, cut into 1-inch cubes

2 teaspoons chopped garlic in water (from 4.5-oz. jar)

1 can (14.5 oz.) diced tomatoes with Italian herbs, undrained

1 1/2 teaspoons dried basil leaves

1/4 cup grated Parmesan cheese

1. Cook linguine as directed on package. Drain; cover to keep warm.

2. Meanwhile, heat 10-inch nonstick skillet over medium-high heat. Add chicken and garlic; cook 5 to 8 minutes, stirring frequently, until chicken is no longer pink in center.

3. Stir in tomatoes and basil. Heat to boiling. Reduce heat to low; cover and simmer 5 minutes, stirring occasionally.

4. Gently stir in cooked linguine. Sprinkle with cheese.

1 Serving: Calories 340 (Calories from Fat 60); Total Fat 6g (Saturated Fat 2.5g; Trans Fat 0g); Cholesterol 80mg; Sodium 720mg; Total Carbohydrate 38g (Dietary Fiber 2g; Sugars 6g); Protein 35g
% Daily Value: Vitamin A 6%; Vitamin C 10%; Calcium 15%; Iron 15%
Exchanges: 2 Starch, 1 Vegetable, 4 Very Lean Meat, 1/2 Fat
Carbohydrate Choices: 2 1/2

sautéed parmesan
chicken SUPER EXPRESS

start to finish **/ 20 MINUTES**

4 servings

1/4 cup all-purpose flour

1/4 cup grated Parmesan cheese

1 teaspoon dried oregano leaves

1 egg, lightly beaten or 1/4 cup fat-free cholesterol-free egg product (from 8-oz. carton)

4 boneless, skinless chicken breasts (1 lb.)

4 teaspoons olive or canola oil

Dash pepper

Dash paprika

1. In shallow dish or pie pan, mix flour, cheese and oregano. In another shallow dish, place egg. Dip each chicken breast into egg; dip into flour mixture to coat, shaking off excess.

2. In 10-inch nonstick skillet, heat oil over medium-high heat 2 to 3 minutes or until very hot. Add chicken; sprinkle with pepper and paprika. Cook 6 minutes. Turn chicken; sprinkle again with pepper and paprika. Cook 6 minutes longer or until chicken is golden brown and juice is no longer pink when center of thickest part is cut (170°F).

1 Serving: Calories 240 (Calories from Fat 90); Total Fat 10g (Saturated Fat 3g; Trans Fat 0g); Cholesterol 75mg; Sodium 210mg; Total Carbohydrate 7g (Dietary Fiber 0g; Sugars 0g); Protein 30g
% Daily Value: Vitamin A 4%; Vitamin C 0%; Calcium 10%; Iron 10%
Exchanges: 1/2 Starch, 4 Very Lean Meat, 1 1/2 Fat
Carbohydrate Choices: 1/2

quick sweet-and-sour
chicken SUPER EXPRESS

start to finish **/ 20 MINUTES**

4 servings (1 cup each)

1 package (3 oz.) chicken-flavor ramen noodle soup mix
3/4 lb. chicken breast strips for stir-fry
1 tablespoon canola or soybean oil
1 cup frozen sugar snap peas (from 1-lb. bag)
1 cup drained baby corn on the cob in water (from 8-oz. can)
2/3 cup sweet-and-sour sauce
2/3 cup water

1. In 1-gallon resealable plastic food-storage bag, place contents of seasoning packet from soup mix. Add chicken strips; seal bag and shake until well coated.

2. Heat oil in 10-inch nonstick skillet or wok over medium-high heat. Add chicken; cook 4 to 5 minutes, stirring frequently, until no longer pink in center.

3. Stir in sugar snap peas, corn, sweet-and-sour sauce and water. Heat to boiling. Cover; cook 3 minutes.

4. Uncover skillet; break noodles apart and add to chicken mixture. Return to boiling. Reduce heat to medium; cover and simmer 3 minutes, stirring occasionally.

1 Serving: Calories 220 (Calories from Fat 70); Total Fat 8g (Saturated Fat 1.5g; Trans Fat 0g); Cholesterol 50mg; Sodium 260mg; Total Carbohydrate 17g (Dietary Fiber 2g; Sugars 10g); Protein 21g
% Daily Value: Vitamin A 4%; Vitamin C 15%; Calcium 4%; Iron 10%
Exchanges: 1 Other Carbohydrate, 3 Very Lean Meat, 1 Fat
Carbohydrate Choices: 1

orange chicken stir-fry SUPER EXPRESS

4 servings (2 1/4 cups each)

"To quickly thaw frozen vegetables, I just place them in a colander or strainer and rinse with warm water until thawed. I make sure I drain them very well."

—Sheila

2 cups uncooked instant rice

2 cups water

3 tablespoons frozen (thawed) orange juice concentrate

2 tablespoons low-sodium soy sauce

1/2 teaspoon cornstarch

1/4 teaspoon garlic powder

1 lb. chicken breast strips for stir-fry

1 bag (1 lb.) frozen broccoli, carrots and water chestnuts, thawed, drained

1. Cook rice in water as directed on package, omitting salt.

2. Meanwhile, in small bowl, mix orange juice concentrate, soy sauce, cornstarch and garlic powder until smooth.

3. Heat 10-inch nonstick skillet over medium-high heat. Add chicken; cook 5 to 8 minutes, stirring frequently, until chicken is no longer pink in center.

4. Stir in juice concentrate mixture and vegetables. Reduce heat to medium; cover and cook 6 to 8 minutes, stirring occasionally, until vegetables are crisp-tender. Serve over rice. If desired, garnish with chopped green onions.

1 Serving: Calories 410 (Calories from Fat 35); Total Fat 4g (Saturated Fat 1g; Trans Fat 0g); Cholesterol 70mg; Sodium 370mg; Total Carbohydrate 61g (Dietary Fiber 4g; Sugars 9g); Protein 31g
% Daily Value: Vitamin A 35%; Vitamin C 35%; Calcium 6%; Iron 15%
Exchanges: 3 Starch, 1/2 Other Carbohydrate, 1 Vegetable, 3 Very Lean Meat
Carbohydrate Choices: 4

chicken
provençal SUPER EXPRESS

4 servings

"My kids are not sold on artichokes, so we'll have them on the side. I like serving this exceptional chicken dish with quick-cooking brown rice."

—Carrie

1 tablespoon olive or canola oil

4 boneless, skinless chicken breasts (1 lb.)

1 large onion, sliced

1 cup cherry tomatoes, halved

1 can (14 oz.) artichoke hearts, drained, quartered

12 pitted extra-large ripe olives, halved

2 cloves garlic, minced

1/2 teaspoon dried rosemary leaves, crushed

1/4 teaspoon fennel seed, crushed

1/2 cup chicken broth

1. In 10-inch nonstick skillet, heat oil over medium heat. Add chicken; cook 4 minutes. Turn chicken; add onion. Cover; cook 3 minutes, stirring occasionally.

2. Stir in remaining ingredients. Reduce heat to medium-low; cover and cook 5 minutes longer or until onion is crisp-tender, vegetables are hot, and juice of chicken is no longer pink when center of thickest part is cut (170°F). If desired, season to taste with salt and pepper.

1 Serving: Calories 260 (Calories from Fat 80); Total Fat 9g (Saturated Fat 2g; Trans Fat 0g); Cholesterol 70mg; Sodium 610mg; Total Carbohydrate 17g (Dietary Fiber 7g; Sugars 4g); Protein 30g
% Daily Value: Vitamin A 10%; Vitamin C 15%; Calcium 8%; Iron 15%
Exchanges: 1 Starch, 1 Vegetable, 3 1/2 Very Lean Meat, 1 Fat
Carbohydrate Choices: 1/2

herb-seasoned
chicken breasts SUPER EXPRESS

start to finish / **20 MINUTES**

4 servings

"These herb-seasoned breasts are great served in whole wheat buns. We might even dip into a barbecue or sweet and sour sauce for added flavor."

—Livia

4 boneless, skinless chicken breasts (1 lb.)
1 teaspoon Italian seasoning
1/2 teaspoon garlic-pepper blend
1/2 teaspoon paprika
1/4 teaspoon salt
1/4 cup chicken broth
1 package (8 oz.) sliced fresh mushrooms (3 cups)

1. Sprinkle both sides of chicken with Italian seasoning, garlic-pepper blend, paprika and salt.

2. Heat 10-inch nonstick skillet over medium heat. Add chicken; cook 3 minutes. Turn chicken; reduce heat to medium-low. Stir in broth and mushrooms. Cover; cook 4 to 7 minutes or until juice of chicken is no longer pink when center of thickest part is cut (170°F).

1 Serving: Calories 150 (Calories from Fat 35); Total Fat 4g (Saturated Fat 1g; Trans Fat 0g); Cholesterol 70mg; Sodium 280mg; Total Carbohydrate 3g (Dietary Fiber 0g; Sugars 0g); Protein 27g
% Daily Value: Vitamin A 4%; Vitamin C 0%; Calcium 2%; Iron 10%
Exchanges: 1 Vegetable, 3 1/2 Very Lean Meat
Carbohydrate Choices: 0

honey mustard–glazed
pork chops SUPER EXPRESS

start to finish **/ 15 MINUTES**

4 servings

1/3 cup honey
2 tablespoons prepared yellow mustard
1/8 teaspoon ground cloves
1/2 teaspoon onion salt
1/4 teaspoon pepper
4 boneless pork loin chops, 3/4 inch thick (1 lb.)
Orange slices, if desired

1. In small bowl, mix honey, mustard and cloves. Sprinkle onion salt and pepper over pork chops.

2. Heat 10-inch nonstick skillet over medium-high heat. Add pork chops; cook 3 minutes. Turn pork. Reduce heat to medium-low; pour honey mixture over pork chops. Cover; cook 5 to 8 minutes longer or until pork is slightly pink in center and thermometer inserted in center of pork reads 160°F. If desired, garnish with orange slices.

---

1 Serving: Calories 310 (Calories from Fat 120); Total Fat 13g (Saturated Fat 4.5g; Trans Fat 0g); Cholesterol 70mg; Sodium 330mg; Total Carbohydrate 24g (Dietary Fiber 0g; Sugars 24g); Protein 23g
% Daily Value: Vitamin A 0%; Vitamin C 0%; Calcium 0%; Iron 6%
Exchanges: 1 1/2 Other Carbohydrate, 3 1/2 Lean Meat, 1/2 Fat
Carbohydrate Choices: 1 1/2

honey mustard–glazed pork chops

pork and pineapple stir-fry SUPER EXPRESS

start to finish / **20 MINUTES**

4 servings (2 cups each)

1 1/2 cups uncooked instant rice

2 cups water

4 tablespoons brown sugar

1 1/2 teaspoons cornstarch

1/2 teaspoon ground ginger

1/4 teaspoon crushed red pepper, if desired

3 tablespoons soy sauce

1 can (20 oz.) pineapple chunks or 16 fresh pineapple chunks, drained, 2 tablespoons liquid reserved

3/4 lb. boneless lean pork, cut into thin bite-size strips

1 bag (16 oz.) coleslaw mix (shredded cabbage and carrots)

1. Cook rice in 1 1/2 cups of the water as directed on package.

2. Meanwhile, in small bowl, mix 3 tablespoons of the brown sugar, the cornstarch, ginger, red pepper, if desired, the remaining 1/2 cup water, the soy sauce and reserved 2 tablespoons pineapple liquid; set aside.

3. Heat 12-inch nonstick skillet over medium-high heat. Add drained pineapple chunks; sprinkle with remaining 1 tablespoon brown sugar. Cook 5 minutes, turning chunks occasionally.

4. Remove pineapple from skillet; set aside. In same skillet, cook and stir pork over medium-high heat 2 minutes.

5. Add coleslaw mix; cook and stir 3 to 6 minutes or until pork is no longer pink in center and cabbage is tender.

6. Stir pineapple and cornstarch mixture into pork mixture; cook and stir 3 minutes or until pork is glazed and sauce is slightly thickened. Serve over rice.

1 Serving: Calories 440 (Calories from Fat 35); Total Fat 4g (Saturated Fat 1.5g; Trans Fat 0g); Cholesterol 55mg; Sodium 760mg; Total Carbohydrate 79g (Dietary Fiber 5g; Sugars 38g); Protein 25g
% Daily Value: Vitamin A 110%; Vitamin C 35%; Calcium 10%; Iron 20%
Exchanges: 2 1/2 Starch, 1 Fruit, 1 1/2 Other Carbohydrate, 2 1/2 Very Lean Meat
Carbohydrate Choices: 5

quick
vegetables

Any one of these versatile veggies provides variety and lots of nutrients, and is done in the same time it takes to prepare the rest of your dinner.

simmerin' squash

Prep: 5 min; Cook: 25 min

    1 large acorn squash (2 lb.)
    1/2 cup apple juice
    1 tablespoon butter or margarine
    1/4 teaspoon ground cinnamon

1   Trim ends off squash. Stand squash on end; cut in half. Remove and discard seeds and fiber. Cut each squash half crosswise into 1/2-inch-thick slices.

2   In 12-inch nonstick skillet, mix apple juice, butter and cinnamon. Add squash; heat to boiling. Reduce heat to low; cover and simmer 10 minutes.

3   Turn squash slices; cover and simmer 5 to 8 minutes or until squash is tender.

4 servings

skin-on mashed potatoes and onions

Prep: 10 min; Cook: 20 min

    3 cups cubed (1 to 1 1/2 inch) unpeeled potatoes
        (1 1/4 lb.)
    1/2 cup plain low-fat yogurt
    1/4 cup shredded Swiss or Gruyère cheese
        (1 oz.)
    2 tablespoons fat-free (skim) milk
    1/2 teaspoon salt
    2 medium green onions, sliced (2 tablespoons)

1   In 3-quart saucepan, place potatoes; add enough water to cover. Heat to boiling. Reduce heat; cover and simmer 15 to 20 minutes or until tender. Drain thoroughly.

2   In same saucepan or large bowl, mash hot potatoes. Beat in yogurt, cheese, milk, salt and pepper until light and fluffy. Stir in onions.

4 servings (3/4 cup each)

orange-glazed carrots

Prep: 20 min

    1 lb. ready-to-eat baby-cut carrots
    1/4 cup slivered almonds
    1/3 cup orange marmalade
    1/2 cup golden raisins

1   In 2-quart saucepan, heat 1/2 cup water to boiling. Add carrots; return to boiling. Reduce heat to medium; cover and cook 10 to 12 minutes, stirring occasionally, until tender.

2   Meanwhile, in 8-inch nonstick skillet, spread almonds in single layer; cook over medium-high heat 4 to 7 minutes, stirring constantly, until lightly browned.

3   Drain carrots; return to saucepan. Stir in marmalade and raisins. Cook over low heat 1 minute, stirring constantly, until marmalade is melted. Gently stir in almonds.

6 servings (1/2 cup each)

orange-glazed carrots

creole-style
skillet dinner SUPER EXPRESS

start to finish / **20 MINUTES**

4 servings (1 3/4 cups each)

"I like to use turkey kielbasa, because it has much less fat and fewer calories than regular kielbasa."

—Margaret

1 medium onion, chopped (1/2 cup)

1/2 medium green bell pepper, chopped (1/2 cup)

1/2 lb. 97%-fat-free smoked turkey kielbasa, quartered lengthwise, sliced

1 can (14.5 oz.) no-salt-added stewed tomatoes

1 1/2 cups water

2 cups uncooked instant rice

Red pepper sauce, if desired

1. Heat 10-inch nonstick skillet over medium-high heat. Add onion and bell pepper; cover and cook, stirring once, until vegetables are crisp-tender.

2. Stir in kielbasa, tomatoes and water. Heat to boiling. Stir in rice; return to boiling. Reduce heat to low; cook about 5 minutes or until rice is tender. Fluff with fork before serving. If desired, serve with red pepper sauce.

1 Serving: Calories 340 (Calories from Fat 50); Total Fat 6g (Saturated Fat 1.5g; Trans Fat 0g); Cholesterol 30mg; Sodium 600mg; Total Carbohydrate 58g (Dietary Fiber 2g; Sugars 7g); Protein 15g
% Daily Value: Vitamin A 8%; Vitamin C 20%; Calcium 6%; Iron 20%
Exchanges: 2 1/2 Starch, 1 Other Carbohydrate, 1 Vegetable, 1 Lean Meat
Carbohydrate Choices: 4

quick family favorites

> "I need really
> quick recipes that
> are good for my
> kids, but it has to
> be something they
> like and will eat."
> —Jeanne A.

SUPER EXPRESS *Ready in 20 minutes or less*

knife and fork
meatball sandwiches

start to finish / **25 MINUTES**

6 sandwiches

3/4 lb. extra-lean (at least 90%) ground beef

1 box (9 oz.) frozen spinach in a pouch, thawed, squeezed and patted dry with paper towels

1 slice whole wheat bread, torn into small pieces

1/2 teaspoon onion powder

1 teaspoon Italian seasoning or 1/2 teaspoon dried oregano leaves

1 egg or 2 egg whites

2 cups reduced-fat tomato pasta sauce

1 loaf (8 oz.) French or Italian bread

1/2 cup shredded mozzarella cheese (2 oz.)

2 tablespoons grated Parmesan cheese

1. Heat oven to 425°F. Line 15 x 10 x 1-inch pan with foil, extending foil over short sides of pan.

2. In medium bowl, mix ground beef, spinach, bread crumbs, onion powder, Italian seasoning and egg. Press mixture into 8 x 6-inch rectangle in pan. Cut rectangle into 36 pieces; do not separate.

3. Bake 10 to 15 minutes or until centers of meatballs are firm and no longer pink and juice is clear. Drain; pat beef with paper towels to remove moisture. With sharp knife, cut into 36 meatballs.

4. Meanwhile, in 3-quart saucepan, heat pasta sauce. Add meatballs; stir to coat.

5. Cut loaf of bread lengthwise to but not through one long side; cut loaf into 6 sections. Place opened sections on individual plates. Spoon 6 meatballs with sauce onto each bread section. Sprinkle with mozzarella and Parmesan cheese. Serve immediately.

1 Sandwich: Calories 340 (Calories from Fat 110); Total Fat 12g (Saturated Fat 4.5g; Trans Fat 0.5g); Cholesterol 80mg; Sodium 800mg; Total Carbohydrate 39g (Dietary Fiber 3g; Sugars 7g); Protein 21g
% Daily Value: Vitamin A 60%; Vitamin C 15%; Calcium 20%; Iron 20%
Exchanges: 2 Starch, 1/2 Other Carbohydrate, 2 Medium-Fat Meat, 1 Fat
Carbohydrate Choices: 2 1/2

italian beef sandwiches

start to finish / **30 MINUTES**

4 sandwiches

3/4 lb. extra-lean (at least 90%) ground beef
2 tablespoons unseasoned dry bread crumbs
1/4 cup fat-free (skim) milk
3/4 teaspoon dried oregano leaves
1/2 teaspoon fennel seed, crushed
1/2 teaspoon garlic powder
1/8 to 1/4 teaspoon crushed red pepper
1 medium onion, halved, thinly sliced
1 medium green bell pepper, thinly sliced
1 tablespoon water
4 whole grain burger buns, split
Mustard, if desired

1. In medium bowl, mix ground beef, bread crumbs, milk, oregano, fennel, garlic powder and red pepper. Shape mixture into 4 patties, 1/2 inch thick.

2. Heat 8-inch nonstick skillet over medium heat. Add onion, bell pepper and water; cover and cook 5 minutes, stirring occasionally, until vegetables are crisp-tender. Remove vegetables from skillet; cover to keep warm.

3. Wipe skillet clean; heat again over medium heat. Add patties; cook 10 to 12 minutes, turning once, until no longer pink in center and juice is clear and thermometer inserted in center of patties reads 160°F. Serve patties and vegetables in buns; if desired, top with mustard.

1 Sandwich: Calories 250 (Calories from Fat 80); Total Fat 9g (Saturated Fat 3g; Trans Fat 0.5g); Cholesterol 55mg; Sodium 270mg; Total Carbohydrate 25g (Dietary Fiber 4g; Sugars 7g); Protein 21g
% Daily Value: Vitamin A 6%; Vitamin C 25%; Calcium 8%; Iron 20%
Exchanges: 1 1/2 Starch, 2 1/2 Lean Meat
Carbohydrate Choices: 1 1/2

sweet 'n easy
sloppy joes SUPER EXPRESS

start to finish **/ 15 MINUTES**

4 sandwiches

> "I keep a lot of
> ingredients in
> my pantry. This
> comes in handy
> because when
> I have to run out
> for something or
> stop at the store
> on my way
> home— that
> takes extra time,
> too."
>
> —Augusto

1/2 lb. extra-lean (at least 90%) ground beef
1/4 cup chopped green bell pepper
3 tablespoons chopped onion
1/4 teaspoon garlic powder
3/4 cup ketchup
1 tablespoon maple-flavored syrup or brown sugar
1 tablespoon Worcestershire sauce
4 whole wheat burger buns, split

1. In 8-inch nonstick skillet, cook ground beef, bell pepper, onion and garlic powder over medium-high heat, stirring frequently, until beef is brown and vegetables are tender; drain.

2. Stir in ketchup, syrup and Worcestershire sauce. Heat to boiling. Reduce heat to medium-low; simmer uncovered 2 minutes. Spoon mixture into buns.

1 Sandwich: Calories 250 (Calories from Fat 60); Total Fat 6g (Saturated Fat 2g; Trans Fat 0.5g); Cholesterol 35mg; Sodium 800mg; Total Carbohydrate 35g (Dietary Fiber 3g; Sugars 18g); Protein 15g
% Daily Value: Vitamin A 15%; Vitamin C 15%; Calcium 4%; Iron 15%
Exchanges: 1 1/2 Starch, 1 Other Carbohydrate, 1 1/2 Lean Meat
Carbohydrate Choices: 2

bumper crop
vegetable soup

start to finish **/ 35 MINUTES**

6 servings (1 1/3 cups each)

3/4 lb. bulk light turkey and pork sausage
2 medium onions, chopped (1 cup)
2 cups cut (1-inch) fresh green beans (8 oz.)
2 cups diced unpeeled potato (about 8 oz.)
4 medium tomatoes, chopped, with juices (2 cups)
1 1/2 cups water
1/4 cup tomato paste
1 can (14 oz.) beef broth

1. Heat nonstick Dutch oven over medium-high heat. Add sausage; cook 4 minutes, stirring frequently. Add onions; cook 2 to 3 minutes, stirring frequently, until onions are tender.

2. Stir in remaining ingredients. Heat to boiling. Reduce heat to low; cover and simmer 15 to 20 minutes or until green beans are tender.

1 Serving: Calories 220 (Calories from Fat 100); Total Fat 11g (Saturated Fat 4g; Trans Fat 0g); Cholesterol 40mg; Sodium 750mg; Total Carbohydrate 19g (Dietary Fiber 4g; Sugars 4g); Protein 13g
% Daily Value: Vitamin A 20%; Vitamin C 20%; Calcium 4%; Iron 15%
Exchanges: 1 Starch, 1 Vegetable, 1 Medium-Fat Meat, 1 Fat
Carbohydrate Choices: 1

sausage, bean and
vegetable soup

start to finish / **40 MINUTES**

5 servings (1 1/2 cups each)

"*I use one or the
other—either
light sausage or
less regular
sausage. A little
goes a long
way—just a little
sausage
heightens the
flavor of this
recipe and keeps
the fat and
calories low.*"

—*Steve*

1/2 lb. bulk light turkey and pork sausage
1/2 medium green bell pepper, finely chopped (1/2 cup)
2 medium zucchini, thinly sliced (1 3/4 cups)
1 medium onion, finely chopped (1/2 cup)
2 cans (14.5 oz. each) no-salt-added stewed tomatoes, undrained, cut up
1 can (15.5 oz.) dark red kidney beans, drained, rinsed
1 can (14 oz.) beef broth
1/2 cup water

1. Heat nonstick Dutch oven or 3-quart saucepan over medium-high heat. Add sausage; cook 4 to 5 minutes, stirring frequently, until no longer pink. Remove sausage from Dutch oven; drain on paper towels. Set aside.

2. Wipe Dutch oven clean with paper towels. Heat Dutch oven again over medium-high heat. Add bell pepper, zucchini and onion; cook 3 minutes.

3. Stir in tomatoes, beans, broth, water and cooked sausage. Heat to boiling. Reduce heat to low; cover tightly and simmer 15 to 18 minutes to blend flavors.

1 Serving: Calories 280 (Calories from Fat 80); Total Fat 9g (Saturated Fat 3g; Trans Fat 0g); Cholesterol 30mg; Sodium 680mg; Total Carbohydrate 34g (Dietary Fiber 8g; Sugars 11g); Protein 19g
% Daily Value: Vitamin A 20%; Vitamin C 30%; Calcium 10%; Iron 25%
Exchanges: 2 Starch, 1/2 Vegetable, 1 1/2 Medium-Fat Meat
Carbohydrate Choices: 2

chicken
noodle soup

5 servings (1 2/3 cups each)

> *"Everyone loves chicken noodle soup. I feel good about making it with my fresh ingredients. It's very soothing served with herbed breadsticks or whole wheat crackers."*
>
> —Anne

1 tablespoon olive or canola oil

3 medium carrots, sliced (1 1/2 cups)

2 medium zucchini, quartered lengthwise, sliced (1 2/3 cups)

1 medium onion, chopped (1/2 cup)

3 boneless, skinless chicken breasts (3/4 lb.), cut into thin bite-size strips

2 cans (14 oz. each) fat-free chicken broth with 1/3 less sodium

1 cup water

1 1/2 cups uncooked fine egg noodles (4 oz.)

1. In nonstick Dutch oven or 3-quart saucepan, heat oil over medium heat. Add carrots, zucchini and onion; cook 5 minutes, stirring frequently.

2. Increase heat to medium-high. Stir in chicken. Cook 3 minutes, stirring frequently. Add broth and water; heat to boiling. Add noodles; boil 3 minutes or until chicken is no longer pink in center and noodles are tender. If desired, season to taste with salt.

1 Serving: Calories 180 (Calories from Fat 50); Total Fat 6g (Saturated Fat 1g; Trans Fat 0g); Cholesterol 50mg; Sodium 420mg; Total Carbohydrate 15g (Dietary Fiber 2g; Sugars 3g); Protein 20g
% Daily Value: Vitamin A 140%; Vitamin C 8%; Calcium 4%; Iron 10%
Exchanges: 1/2 Starch, 1 Vegetable, 2 1/2 Very Lean Meat, 1/2 Fat
Carbohydrate Choices: 1

chicken and
pasta chowder

6 servings (1 2/3 cups each)

"I look for ways to add milk and veggies to our dinners, because my son does not like to drink milk and he's more likely to eat veggies if they are in soup."

—Kelly

3 boneless, skinless chicken breasts (3/4 lb.), cut into bite-size pieces

1 medium onion, chopped (1/2 cup)

2 cloves garlic, minced

2 cans (14 oz. each) chicken or vegetable broth

1 teaspoon dried basil leaves

3/4 cup uncooked rotini pasta (2.5 oz.)

1 bag (1 lb.) frozen broccoli, carrots and cauliflower

4 cups fat-free (skim) milk

1/2 cup all-purpose flour

1/2 medium red bell pepper, chopped (1/2 cup)

1/4 cup shredded Parmesan cheese (1 oz.)

1. Heat nonstick Dutch oven or 3-quart nonstick saucepan over medium heat. Add chicken, onion and garlic; cook 4 to 6 minutes, stirring occasionally, until onion is tender.

2. Stir in broth, basil and salt. Heat to boiling. Increase heat to medium-high. Add pasta; cook 8 minutes, stirring occasionally.

3. Meanwhile, place frozen vegetables in colander or strainer; rinse with warm water until thawed. Drain well. In small bowl, mix 1 cup of the milk and the flour until smooth.

4. Stir vegetables, milk mixture, remaining 3 cups milk and the bell pepper into pasta mixture. Heat just to boiling, stirring frequently. Reduce heat to medium; cook 3 to 5 minutes, stirring occasionally, until soup thickens, vegetables and pasta are tender and chicken is no longer pink in center. Sprinkle individual servings with cheese.

1 Serving: Calories 280 (Calories from Fat 40); Total Fat 4.5g (Saturated Fat 2g; Trans Fat 0g); Cholesterol 40mg; Sodium 770mg; Total Carbohydrate 34g (Dietary Fiber 4g; Sugars 10g); Protein 27g
% Daily Value: Vitamin A 60%; Vitamin C 45%; Calcium 30%; Iron 15%
Exchanges: 2 Starch, 1 Vegetable, 2 1/2 Very Lean Meat, 1/2 Fat
Carbohydrate Choices: 2

tortilla and cheese chili

4 servings (1 1/2 cups each)

"*I try to speed up making dinner by gathering all the ingredients I need and measuring them the morning or evening before.*"

—Anne

1/2 lb. extra-lean (at least 90%) ground beef

2 medium onions, chopped (1 cup)

4 medium tomatoes, finely chopped (3 cups)

2 cups reduced-sodium beef broth

2 tablespoons chili powder

1 tablespoon ketchup

4 soft corn tortillas, cut into 1 x 1/2-inch strips

1/2 cup shredded reduced-fat sharp Cheddar cheese (2 oz.)

1. Heat 2-quart nonstick saucepan over medium-high heat. Add ground beef and onions; cook 4 to 6 minutes, stirring frequently, until beef is brown and onions are tender.

2. Stir in tomatoes, broth, chili powder and ketchup. Heat to boiling. Reduce heat to medium-low; cover and simmer 5 minutes. Increase heat to medium. Uncover; cook 5 minutes longer.

3. Stir in tortilla strips until thoroughly coated. Cover; cook 3 minutes. Top individual servings with cheese.

1 Serving: Calories 240 (Calories from Fat 70); Total Fat 8g (Saturated Fat 3g; Trans Fat 0g); Cholesterol 40mg; Sodium 380mg; Total Carbohydrate 26g (Dietary Fiber 5g; Sugars 6g); Protein 20g
% Daily Value: Vitamin A 50%; Vitamin C 25%; Calcium 20%; Iron 15%
Exchanges: 1 Starch, 1/2 Other Carbohydrate, 1 Vegetable, 2 Lean Meat
Carbohydrate Choices: 1 1/2

sausage and cheese
pasta *SUPER EXPRESS*

start to finish / **20 MINUTES**

6 servings (1 1/3 cups each)

4 cups uncooked medium pasta shells (9 oz.)

2 cups frozen cut green beans (from 1-lb. bag)

1 1/2 cups fat-free (skim) milk

3 tablespoons all-purpose flour

1/2 cup reduced-fat process cheese sauce (from a jar)

6 oz. reduced-fat smoked turkey sausage, halved lengthwise, sliced (about 1 cup)

1. In 3-quart saucepan, cook pasta as directed on package 2 minutes. Add green beans; return to boiling. Cook 8 to 10 minutes or until pasta and beans are tender. Drain; return to saucepan.

2. Meanwhile, in 10-inch nonstick skillet, mix milk and flour until smooth. Heat to boiling over medium-high heat, stirring constantly. Cook and stir until thickened. Remove from heat.

3. Stir in cheese sauce and sausage until cheese sauce is melted. Add cooked pasta and beans; toss gently to coat. Reduce heat to medium-low; cook until thoroughly heated.

1 Serving: Calories 310 (Calories from Fat 80); Total Fat 9g (Saturated Fat 4.5g; Trans Fat 0g); Cholesterol 30mg; Sodium 690mg; Total Carbohydrate 45g (Dietary Fiber 4g; Sugars 7g); Protein 15g
% Daily Value: Vitamin A 10%; Vitamin C 0%; Calcium 20%; Iron 15%
Exchanges: 2 1/2 Starch, 1 Vegetable, 1 Medium-Fat Meat, 1/2 Fat
Carbohydrate Choices: 3

skillet
shepherd's pie

start to finish / **40 MINUTES**

4 servings (1 1/2 cups each)

"I use extra-lean ground beef and ground turkey interchangeably. So I might use lean ground beef in this easy skillet dish; it depends what I have on hand."

—Nancy

1 lb. lean ground turkey
1 cup coarsely chopped carrots
1 cup coarsely chopped celery
1 medium onion, chopped (1/2 cup)
1 can (10.75 oz.) reduced-fat and reduced-sodium cream of mushroom soup
1/4 cup beef broth
1 1/3 cups water
1/2 cup fat-free sour cream
1 1/3 cups plain mashed potato mix (dry)
2 tablespoons chopped fresh parsley or 2 teaspoons dried parsley flakes

1. In 10-inch nonstick skillet, cook ground turkey, carrots, celery and onion over medium-high heat, stirring frequently, until turkey is no longer pink. If necessary, drain.

2. Stir in soup and broth. Reduce heat to low; cover and simmer 15 minutes, stirring occasionally.

3. Meanwhile, in 2-quart saucepan, heat water to boiling. Remove from heat. Stir in sour cream and mashed potato mix until desired consistency. Stir in parsley.

4. Spoon large dollops of potato mixture over turkey mixture in skillet. Cover; cook about 5 minutes or until potatoes are thoroughly heated.

1 Serving: Calories 470 (Calories from Fat 70); Total Fat 8g (Saturated Fat 2g; Trans Fat 0g); Cholesterol 80mg; Sodium 410mg; Total Carbohydrate 71g (Dietary Fiber 7g; Sugars 6g); Protein 32g
% Daily Value: Vitamin A 120%; Vitamin C 30%; Calcium 10%; Iron 15%
Exchanges: 3 1/2 Starch, 1 Other Carbohydrate, 3 Very Lean Meat, 1 Fat
Carbohydrate Choices: 4

home-style sausage and potato skillet

start to finish **/ 50 MINUTES**

4 servings (1 1/4 cups each)

3/4 lb. bulk light turkey and pork sausage
2 medium onions, chopped (1 cup)
2 lb. red potatoes (about 12 medium), unpeeled, very thinly sliced
1 cup water
1/2 teaspoon salt
1/2 teaspoon paprika
1/4 teaspoon dried thyme leaves
1/8 teaspoon pepper

1. Heat nonstick Dutch oven over medium-high heat. Add sausage; cook 4 to 5 minutes, stirring frequently, until no longer pink. Remove sausage from Dutch oven; drain on paper towels. Set aside.

2. Wipe Dutch oven clean with paper towels. Add onions; cook over medium heat about 5 minutes, stirring occasionally.

3. Gently stir in cooked sausage and remaining ingredients. Heat to boiling. Reduce heat to medium-low; cover tightly and cook 8 to 10 minutes, stirring occasionally, just until potatoes are tender.

4. Remove Dutch oven from heat; gently stir mixture. Let stand covered 10 minutes to allow flavors to blend and light sauce to form.

---

1 Serving: Calories 390 (Calories from Fat 140); Total Fat 16g (Saturated Fat 6g; Trans Fat 0g); Cholesterol 60mg; Sodium 860mg; Total Carbohydrate 45g (Dietary Fiber 6g; Sugars 4g); Protein 19g
% Daily Value: Vitamin A 6%; Vitamin C 25%; Calcium 6%; Iron 30%
Exchanges: 3 Starch, 1 1/2 Medium-Fat Meat, 1 Fat
Carbohydrate Choices: 2 1/2

home-style sausage and potato skillet

beef dinner
nachos SUPER EXPRESS

start to finish / **15 MINUTES**

6 servings

1/2 lb. extra-lean (at least 90%) ground beef
1 can (15 or 15.5 oz.) pinto beans, drained, rinsed
1 package (1.25 oz.) 40%-less-sodium taco seasoning mix
1/3 cup water
3 1/2 cups reduced-fat nacho cheese tortilla chips (3 oz.)
1/2 cup shredded reduced-fat Colby-Monterey Jack cheese blend (2 oz.)
1 medium tomato, chopped (3/4 cup)
1 cup shredded leaf lettuce
1/2 cup fat-free sour cream
2 tablespoons chopped fresh cilantro

1. In 10-inch nonstick skillet, cook ground beef over medium-high heat, stirring frequently, until brown; drain. Stir in beans, taco seasoning mix and water. Heat to boiling. Reduce heat to medium-low; simmer uncovered 1 to 2 minutes or until water is absorbed.

2. Arrange tortilla chips evenly on individual plates. Spoon beef mixture evenly over chips. Top with cheese, tomato, lettuce, sour cream and cilantro.

1 Serving: Calories 240 (Calories from Fat 50); Total Fat 5g (Saturated Fat 2.5g; Trans Fat 0g); Cholesterol 30mg; Sodium 560mg; Total Carbohydrate 36g (Dietary Fiber 6g; Sugars 2g); Protein 17g
% Daily Value: Vitamin A 15%; Vitamin C 8%; Calcium 15%; Iron 20%
Exchanges: 2 1/2 Starch, 1 1/2 Very Lean Meat, 1/2 Fat
Carbohydrate Choices: 2

beef tenderloin with mushroom-shallot sauce SUPER EXPRESS

start to finish / **20 MINUTES**

2 servings

"Using beef tenderloin is great because it is very lean and we're trying to cut back on fat and calories. Though we want to eat less meat, we still like to have it once in a while."

—Greg

2 beef tenderloin steaks (filet mignon) (1/2 lb.)
1 large clove garlic, peeled, halved
1/4 teaspoon coarse ground black pepper
1 teaspoon butter or margarine
1 cup fresh whole mushrooms, halved
2 shallots, thinly sliced
1/4 cup Cabernet Sauvignon or other dry red wine
1/4 cup beef broth
1 teaspoon cornstarch

1. Set oven control to broil. Line 15 x 10-inch pan with sides with foil. Rub both sides of each steak with cut side of garlic. Sprinkle each side with pepper; place steaks in pan.

2. Broil 4 to 6 inches from heat 12 to 16 minutes, turning once, until desired doneness.

3. Meanwhile, in 7-inch nonstick skillet, melt butter over medium heat. Add mushrooms and shallots; cook 4 to 6 minutes, stirring frequently, until shallots are tender and mushrooms begin to brown. Add wine; cook 1 minute, stirring occasionally.

4. In small bowl, mix broth and cornstarch until smooth. Gradually stir into mushroom mixture, cooking and stirring until bubbly and thickened. Serve sauce over steaks.

1 Serving: Calories 210 (Calories from Fat 90); Total Fat 10g (Saturated Fat 4g; Trans Fat 0g); Cholesterol 70mg; Sodium 200mg; Total Carbohydrate 5g (Dietary Fiber 0g; Sugars 0g); Protein 26g
% Daily Value: Vitamin A 4%; Vitamin C 2%; Calcium 2%; Iron 15%
Exchanges: 1/2 Starch, 3 1/2 Lean Meat
Carbohydrate Choices: 1/2

beef with
burgundy mushrooms

4 servings

2 cups uncooked medium egg noodles (4 oz.)

1 lb. boneless beef sirloin steak (1/2 inch thick), cut into 4 pieces

2 packages (8 oz. each) fresh whole mushrooms, quartered

1 can (10.5 oz.) condensed French onion soup

1/4 cup Burgundy or other dry red wine

1 tablespoon cornstarch

3 tablespoons tomato paste with basil, garlic and oregano

1/2 teaspoon dried oregano leaves

2 tablespoons chopped fresh parsley

Pepper

1. Cook and drain noodles as directed on package, omitting salt. Place in serving bowl; cover to keep warm.

2. Meanwhile, heat 12-inch nonstick skillet over medium-high heat. Add beef; cook 3 to 4 minutes on each side or until desired doneness. Remove from heat. Place beef on serving platter; cover to keep warm.

3. Wipe skillet clean with paper towels. Heat skillet again over medium-high heat. Add mushrooms; cook 10 minutes, stirring occasionally.

4. Meanwhile, in medium bowl, mix soup, wine, cornstarch, tomato paste and oregano.

5. Add soup mixture to mushrooms; cook, stirring frequently, until bubbly and thickened. Remove from heat. Stir in parsley and season to taste with pepper. Spoon mushroom mixture over beef; serve with noodles.

1 Serving: Calories 310 (Calories from Fat 60); Total Fat 7g (Saturated Fat 2g; Trans Fat 0g); Cholesterol 85mg; Sodium 730mg; Total Carbohydrate 33g (Dietary Fiber 4g; Sugars 3g); Protein 32g
% Daily Value: Vitamin A 10%; Vitamin C 10%; Calcium 4%; Iron 30%
Exchanges: 2 Starch, 3 1/2 Very Lean Meat, 1 Fat
Carbohydrate Choices: 2

beef with burgundy mushrooms

spicy broccoli-beef stir-fry

start to finish **/ 25 MINUTES**

4 servings (1 3/4 cups each)

"When a recipe calls for thinly sliced meat, I've found that it works better to slice the beef while it is still partially frozen."

—Kim

8 oz. uncooked vermicelli

1/2 cup orange juice

1 tablespoon cornstarch

2 tablespoons soy sauce

2 teaspoons sugar

3/4 teaspoon five-spice powder

1/8 to 1/4 teaspoon crushed red pepper

3/4 lb. boneless beef sirloin steak, cut into thin bite-size strips

1 medium onion, cut into 16 wedges

1 clove garlic, minced

3 cups fresh broccoli florets (about 6 oz.)

1 small red bell pepper, cut into thin bite-size strips (about 1 cup)

1. Cook vermicelli as directed on package. Drain; cover to keep warm.

2. Meanwhile, in small bowl, mix orange juice, cornstarch, soy sauce, sugar, five-spice powder and red pepper until well blended; set aside.

3. Heat 10-inch nonstick skillet or wok over medium-high heat. Add beef, onion and garlic; cook and stir 3 to 5 minutes or until beef is desired doneness and onion is crisp-tender.

4. Add broccoli and bell pepper; cover and cook 2 to 4 minutes, stirring occasionally, until vegetables are crisp-tender. Add cornstarch mixture; cook and stir 2 to 3 minutes or until bubbly and thickened. Serve over vermicelli.

1 Serving: Calories 370 (Calories from Fat 35); Total Fat 4g (Saturated Fat 1g; Trans Fat 0g); Cholesterol 45mg; Sodium 740mg; Total Carbohydrate 61g (Dietary Fiber 7g; Sugars 10g); Protein 28g
% Daily Value: Vitamin A 45%; Vitamin C 100%; Calcium 6%; Iron 25%
Exchanges: 3 Starch, 1/2 Other Carbohydrate, 2 Vegetable, 2 Very Lean Meat
Carbohydrate Choices: 3 1/2

turkey and
penne pasta

start to finish **/ 25 MINUTES**

4 servings (1 2/3 cups each)

2 cups uncooked penne pasta (8 oz.)
1/2 lb. lean ground turkey
2 cloves garlic, minced
1/2 teaspoon Italian seasoning
1/4 teaspoon fennel seed, crushed, if desired
2 cups fat-free extra-chunky tomato pasta sauce
1/4 teaspoon sugar
1/2 cup finely shredded or shredded mozzarella cheese (2 oz.)

1. Cook pasta as directed on package. Drain; cover to keep warm.

2. Meanwhile, heat 10-inch nonstick skillet or Dutch oven over medium-high heat. Add turkey, garlic, Italian seasoning and fennel, if desired; cook 3 to 5 minutes, stirring frequently, until turkey is no longer pink.

3. Stir in pasta sauce and sugar. Heat to boiling. Reduce heat to low; cover and simmer 10 minutes to blend flavors. Serve sauce over pasta; sprinkle with mozzarella cheese.

1 Serving: Calories 460 (Calories from Fat 100); Total Fat 11g (Saturated Fat 3.5g; Trans Fat 0g); Cholesterol 45mg; Sodium 730mg; Total Carbohydrate 69g (Dietary Fiber 5g; Sugars 10g); Protein 25g
% Daily Value: Vitamin A 20%; Vitamin C 15%; Calcium 15%; Iron 20%
Exchanges: 3 1/2 Starch, 1 Other Carbohydrate, 2 Lean Meat, 1/2 Fat
Carbohydrate Choices: 4

turkey
meat loaves

start to finish / **40 MINUTES**

6 servings (2 loaves each)

"Smaller amounts take less time to bake. Baking these turkey meat loaves in muffin cups cuts the bake time in half, and my kids love having their own individual servings."

—Cheri

1 1/2 lb. ground turkey breast
3/4 cup old-fashioned or quick-cooking oats
1 small red bell pepper, finely chopped
1/2 cup apple juice
3 teaspoons onion powder
1 teaspoon salt
1 teaspoon dried sage leaves, crushed
1/2 teaspoon pepper
1/4 teaspoon garlic powder
2 tablespoons apple juice

1. Heat oven to 375°F. Spray 12 regular-size muffin cups with cooking spray. In medium bowl, mix all ingredients except 2 tablespoons apple juice.

2. Spoon mixture evenly into muffin cups, mounding tops. Brush tops with 2 tablespoons apple juice.

3. Bake 20 to 30 minutes or until thermometer inserted in center of loaf reads 165°F.

1 Serving: Calories 210 (Calories from Fat 60); Total Fat 7g (Saturated Fat 2g; Trans Fat 0g); Cholesterol 75mg; Sodium 470mg; Total Carbohydrate 12g (Dietary Fiber 1g; Sugars 4g); Protein 27g
% Daily Value: Vitamin A 15%; Vitamin C 20%; Calcium 2%; Iron 10%
Exchanges: 1/2 Starch, 3 1/2 Very Lean Meat, 1 Fat
Carbohydrate Choices: 1

turkey meat loaves

turkey scallopini with
lemon sauce SUPER EXPRESS

start to finish / **15 MINUTES**

6 servings

"Couscous is the perfect pasta for fast dinners because it is so small and cooks in no time. Another benefit: my kids just love it!"

— Cheri

Couscous
1 cup uncooked couscous
1 1/2 cups water

Sauce
2 teaspoons all-purpose flour
1/4 teaspoon salt
1/8 teaspoon dried thyme leaves
1 cup fat-free (skim) milk
1 teaspoon all natural butter-flavor granules
1/4 teaspoon grated lemon peel

Turkey
6 uncooked turkey breast slices (about 1 lb.)
1/4 teaspoon salt
1/8 teaspoon pepper
1 tablespoon butter or margarine
2 tablespoons chopped fresh parsley

1. Cook couscous in water as directed on package, omitting oil; cover to keep warm.

2. Meanwhile, in 1-quart saucepan, mix flour, 1/4 teaspoon salt, the thyme and milk until smooth. Cook over medium-high heat, stirring constantly, until bubbly and thickened. Remove from heat. Stir in butter-flavor granules and lemon peel until well blended; cover to keep warm.

3. Sprinkle both sides of turkey breast slices with 1/4 teaspoon salt and the pepper. In 10-inch nonstick skillet, melt butter over medium-high heat. Add turkey; cook 2 to 3 minutes, turning once, until no longer pink in center. Serve turkey slices with sauce over couscous; sprinkle with parsley.

1 Serving: Calories 210 (Calories from Fat 25); Total Fat 3g (Saturated Fat 1.5g; Trans Fat 0g);
Cholesterol 55mg; Sodium 300mg; Total Carbohydrate 25g (Dietary Fiber 2g; Sugars 2g); Protein 23g
% Daily Value: Vitamin A 6%; Vitamin C 0%; Calcium 8%; Iron 8%
Exchanges: 1 1/2 Starch, 2 1/2 Very Lean Meat
Carbohydrate Choices: 1 1/2

easy chicken
tetrazzini SUPER EXPRESS

start to finish **/ 20 MINUTES**

4 servings (1 1/4 cups each)

1 package (7 oz.) spaghetti, broken into thirds
1 tablespoon butter or margarine
8 medium green onions, sliced (1/2 cup)
1 package (8 oz.) sliced fresh mushrooms (3 cups)
3 tablespoons all-purpose flour
1/4 teaspoon garlic powder
1/8 teaspoon pepper
1 cup chicken broth
1/2 cup fat-free (skim) milk
2 cups cubed cooked chicken
1 jar (2 oz.) sliced pimientos, drained
2 tablespoons dry sherry
1/4 cup grated Parmesan cheese

1. In 3-quart saucepan, cook spaghetti as directed on package. Drain in colander; set aside.

2. In same saucepan, melt butter over medium-high heat. Add onions and mushrooms; cook, stirring frequently, until tender. In small bowl, mix flour, garlic powder, pepper, broth and milk until smooth. Gradually stir into onion mixture, cooking and stirring until bubbly and thickened.

3. Stir in chicken, pimientos and sherry. Cook, stirring occasionally, until thoroughly heated. Stir in cheese. Add cooked spaghetti; toss gently. If desired, serve with additional grated Parmesan cheese and chopped fresh parsley.

1 Serving: Calories 430 (Calories from Fat 100); Total Fat 11g (Saturated Fat 4.5g; Trans Fat 0g); Cholesterol 75mg; Sodium 670mg; Total Carbohydrate 50g (Dietary Fiber 4g; Sugars 4g); Protein 34g
% Daily Value: Vitamin A 15%; Vitamin C 15%; Calcium 15%; Iron 25%
Exchanges: 3 Starch, 1 Vegetable, 3 Lean Meat
Carbohydrate Choices: 3

quick family favorites **97**

mandarin orange
chicken

6 *servings*

"Flattening the chicken breasts takes a little time, but is well worth it because it shaves off minutes during cooking."

— *Sharon*

6 boneless, skinless chicken breasts (1 1/2 lb.)

1 1/2 teaspoons dried basil leaves

1/4 teaspoon salt

Dash ground red pepper (cayenne)

1 tablespoon butter or margarine

1 medium onion, finely chopped (1/2 cup)

1/2 cup chicken broth

1 can (11 oz.) mandarin orange segments, drained, 2 tablespoons liquid reserved

1 teaspoon cornstarch

1. To flatten each chicken breast, place between 2 sheets of plastic wrap or waxed paper. Working from center, pound chicken with flat side of meat mallet or rolling pin until about 1/2 inch thick; remove wrap. Sprinkle chicken with basil, salt and ground red pepper.

2. In 10-inch nonstick skillet, melt butter over medium-high heat. Add chicken; cook 5 minutes. Turn chicken; add onion. Cook 4 to 6 minutes longer or until juice of chicken is no longer pink when center of thickest part is cut (170°F).

3. In small bowl, mix broth, reserved 2 tablespoons mandarin orange liquid and the cornstarch until smooth. Add to chicken in skillet; cook and stir until bubbly and thickened. Gently stir in orange segments; cook until thoroughly heated.

1 Serving: Calories 180 (Calories from Fat 50); Total Fat 6g (Saturated Fat 2g; Trans Fat 0g); Cholesterol 75mg; Sodium 260mg; Total Carbohydrate 7g (Dietary Fiber 0g; Sugars 5g); Protein 26g
% Daily Value: Vitamin A 15%; Vitamin C 15%; Calcium 2%; Iron 6%
Exchanges: 1/2 Other Carbohydrate, 3 1/2 Very Lean Meat, 1/2 Fat
Carbohydrate Choices: 1/2

chicken parmesan
italiano

start to finish **/ 30 MINUTES**

4 servings

"I look for ways to cook that don't add extra fat. This is a great one because the Parmesan-crumb crust keeps the chicken moist and adds great flavor."

— Livia

1/4 cup Italian-style dry bread crumbs
1/4 cup shredded Parmesan cheese
1 teaspoon dried oregano leaves
2 tablespoons lemon juice
2 small cloves garlic, minced
4 boneless, skinless chicken breasts (1 lb.)
Cooking spray

1. Heat oven to 425°F. Line cookie sheet with foil; spray foil with cooking spray.

2. In shallow dish, mix bread crumbs, cheese and oregano. In small cup or bowl, mix lemon juice and garlic. Brush both sides of each chicken breast with lemon juice mixture; coat with bread crumb mixture. Place on cookie sheet. Lightly spray chicken with cooking spray.

3. Bake 15 to 20 minutes or until juice of chicken is no longer pink when center of thickest part is cut (170°F).

1 Serving: Calories 200 (Calories from Fat 60); Total Fat 7g (Saturated Fat 2.5g; Trans Fat 0g); Cholesterol 75mg; Sodium 240mg; Total Carbohydrate 6g (Dietary Fiber 0g; Sugars 0g); Protein 28g
% Daily Value: Vitamin A 0%; Vitamin C 2%; Calcium 10%; Iron 8%
Exchanges: 1/2 Other Carbohydrate, 4 Very Lean Meat, 1 Fat
Carbohydrate Choices: 1/2

healthy
holidays

Want your holidays to be healthy and happy? People are often look-ing for lower-fat recipes during the holidays. With these sensational, super-easy appetizers and dessert, look no further!

cream cheese with ginger-chile sauce

Prep 10 min

> 1/3 cup apricot preserves
> 1/2 **each** red and green jalapeño chile, seeded, finely chopped
> 1 teaspoon grated gingerroot or 1/4 teaspoon ground ginger
> 1 teaspoon cider vinegar
> 1 package (8 oz.) 1/3-less-fat cream cheese (Neufchâtel), well chilled
> 24 fat-free crackers
> Whole green chile

1   In small bowl, mix preserves, 1/2 red and 1/2 green chopped chilies, gingerroot and vinegar until well blended.

2   Cut cream cheese diagonally from one corner to the oppo-site corner. On serving plate or tray, place long sides of cheese together forming a triangle or tree shape.

3   Top cheese with preserves mixture. Place 1 small whole green chile at base for tree trunk. Serve with crackers.

8 servings (3 tablespoons spread and 3 crackers each)

raspberry sherbet pie

Prep: 15 min; Freeze: 1 hr

> **Crust**
> 1 1/2 cups graham cracker crumbs
> 1 tablespoon sugar
> 3/4 teaspoon ground cinnamon
> 3 tablespoons butter or margarine, melted
>
> **Filling**
> 1 quart (4 cups) raspberry sherbet, softened
> 2 tablespoons semisweet chocolate chips
> 2 teaspoons milk
> Fresh raspberries and mint leaves, if desired

1   Heat oven to 375°F. Mix crust ingredients; press in bottom and up side of 9-inch pie pan. Bake 8 to 10 minutes or until light golden brown. Cool about 20 minutes.

2   Spoon sherbet into cooled baked crust. In 1-quart saucepan, heat chocolate chips and milk over low heat, stirring constantly, until chocolate is melted and mixture is smooth. Drizzle over sherbet. Freeze 30 to 60 minutes, until firm. If desired, garnish with raspberries and mint.

8 servings

molded herbed cheese spread with apples

Prep: 20 min; Chill: 2 hr

> 1 container (12 oz.) fat-free cream cheese (1 1/2 cups), softened
> 2 oz. feta cheese, crumbled (1/2 cup)
> 1 oz. blue cheese, crumbled (1/4 cup)
> 1/2 teaspoon dried basil leaves
> 1/2 teaspoon dried rosemary leaves, crushed
> 1 tablespoon finely chopped fresh chives or green onion tops
> 2 red or green apples, cut into 16 slices each, or assorted fat-free crackers

1   Line 2-cup ring mold or small decorative mold with cheesecloth or plastic wrap.

2   In medium bowl, beat cream cheese, feta cheese, blue cheese, basil and rosemary with electric mixer or spoon until well mixed. Spoon mixture into mold, spreading evenly. Cover with plastic wrap; refrigerate about 2 hours, until firm.

3   To serve, unmold cheese mixture onto serving platter; sprinkle with chives. Serve with apple slices.

16 servings (2 tablespoons spread and 2 apple slices each)

cream cheese with ginger-chile sauce

springtime
chicken stir-fry

4 servings (1 1/4 cups each)

1 package (3 oz.) chicken-flavor ramen noodle soup mix
1/4 cup water
1/4 cup garlic-ginger stir-fry sauce
4 boneless, skinless chicken thighs (about 3/4 lb.), cut into bite-size pieces
2 cloves garlic, minced
1 large carrot, cut diagonally into thin slices
1/2 medium red onion (halved lengthwise), cut into thin wedges
2 cups fresh sugar snap peas (1/2 lb.), trimmed

1. In 2-quart saucepan, heat 2 cups water to boiling. If desired, break ramen noodles into pieces. Add noodles to boiling water; cook 2 minutes, stirring occasionally. Drain.

2. In small bowl, mix contents of seasoning packet from soup mix, 1/4 cup water and the stir-fry sauce until well blended; set aside.

3. Heat 10-inch nonstick skillet or wok over medium-high heat. Add chicken and garlic; cook and stir 2 minutes. Add carrot and onion; cook and stir 3 minutes longer or until chicken is no longer pink in center.

4. Add sugar snap peas and sauce mixture; cook and stir until bubbly. Reduce heat to medium-low; stir in cooked noodles. Cook until thoroughly heated.

1 Serving: Calories 260 (Calories from Fat 100); Total Fat 11g (Saturated Fat 3.5g; Trans Fat 1.5g); Cholesterol 55mg; Sodium 730mg; Total Carbohydrate 21g (Dietary Fiber 3g; Sugars 5g); Protein 23g
% Daily Value: Vitamin A 70%; Vitamin C 25%; Calcium 6%; Iron 20%
Exchanges: 1 Starch, 1 Vegetable, 2 1/2 Lean Meat, 1/2 Fat
Carbohydrate Choices: 1 1/2

lemon butter
catfish fillets SUPER EXPRESS

start to finish / **20 MINUTES**

4 servings

1 lb. catfish fillets

1 cup water

2 teaspoons cornstarch

1/2 teaspoon chicken bouillon granules

Dash pepper

2 tablespoons all-natural butter-flavor granules

1 teaspoon grated lemon peel

1 tablespoon chopped fresh chives

1. Set oven control to broil. Line 15 x 10-inch pan with sides with foil; spray foil with cooking spray. Pat catfish fillets dry with paper towels; place in pan.

2. Broil 4 to 6 inches from heat 8 to 10 minutes, turning once, until fish flakes easily with fork.

3. Meanwhile, in 1-quart saucepan, mix water, cornstarch, bouillon and pepper until smooth. Cook over medium heat, stirring frequently, until bubbly and thickened. Reduce heat to low; stir in butter-flavor granules and lemon peel. Remove from heat; stir in chives. Serve sauce over fish.

1 Serving: Calories 170 (Calories from Fat 70); Total Fat 7g (Saturated Fat 1.5g; Trans Fat 0g); Cholesterol 85mg; Sodium 440mg; Total Carbohydrate 3g (Dietary Fiber 0g; Sugars 0g); Protein 23g
% Daily Value: Vitamin A 0%; Vitamin C 2%; Calcium 6%; Iron 10%
Exchanges: 3 Lean Meat
Carbohydrate Choices: 0

lemon butter catfish fillets

crispy oven-baked fish

start to finish **/ 30 MINUTES**

2 servings

1 egg or 1 egg white
1 teaspoon water
1/3 cup Italian-style dry bread crumbs
1/2 teaspoon lemon-pepper seasoning
1/4 teaspoon garlic salt
2 catfish or tilapia fillets (3 to 4 oz. each)
Cooking spray
4 lemon wedges

1. Heat oven to 400°F. Line cookie sheet with foil; generously spray foil with cooking spray. In shallow bowl or dish, beat egg and water with wire whisk until well blended. In another shallow bowl or dish, mix bread crumbs, lemon-pepper seasoning and garlic salt.

2. Dip fish into egg mixture; coat with bread crumb mixture. Place on cookie sheet. Spray fish with cooking spray.

3. Bake 10 minutes. Turn fillets; bake 5 to 10 minutes longer or until fish flakes easily with fork. Place fillets on serving platter; garnish with lemon wedges.

1 Serving: Calories 280 (Calories from Fat 110); Total Fat 12g (Saturated Fat 2.5g; Trans Fat 0g); Cholesterol 190mg; Sodium 460mg; Total Carbohydrate 15g (Dietary Fiber 0g; Sugars 2g); Protein 29g
% Daily Value: Vitamin A 4%; Vitamin C 8%; Calcium 10%; Iron 20%
Exchanges: 1 Starch, 4 Lean Meat
Carbohydrate Choices: 1

crispy oven-baked fish

fish and rice bundles

start to finish **/ 35 MINUTES**

4 servings

> *"We're trying to eat more fish. This recipe is really fun and very quick. I'd add colorful, fresh veggies like cucumber slices, green pepper strips or baby carrots for crunch."*
>
> —Christian

1 box (6.25 oz.) quick-cooking white and wild rice mix
4 sole or flounder fillets, each about 9 x 4 inches (3/4 to 1 lb.)
Paprika
Lemon wedges, if desired

1. Heat oven to 450°F. Line 15 x 10-inch pan with sides with foil. Cook rice as directed on box.

2. Spoon 3/4 cup cooked rice mixture down center of each sole fillet. Starting at narrow end, roll up each; secure with toothpick. With pancake turner, place roll-ups in pan. Sprinkle lightly with paprika. Cover loosely with foil.

3. Bake 15 to 20 minutes or until fish flakes easily with fork. If desired, garnish with lemon wedges.

1 Serving: Calories 160 (Calories from Fat 10); Total Fat 1g (Saturated Fat 0g; Trans Fat 0g); Cholesterol 40mg; Sodium 340mg; Total Carbohydrate 20g (Dietary Fiber 0g; Sugars 0g); Protein 16g
% Daily Value: Vitamin A 0%; Vitamin C 0%; Calcium 0%; Iron 6%
Exchanges: 1 1/2 Starch, 1 1/2 Very Lean Meat
Carbohydrate Choices: 1

classic
pizza

8 servings

"Pizza—my family's favorite. And it's so easy to make at home, who needs take-out? I feel better knowing I am adding my own fresh ingredients."

—Cheri

1 can (13.8 oz.) refrigerated pizza crust
1/2 lb. bulk light turkey and pork sausage
1 can (14.5 oz.) stewed tomatoes, drained
1/2 teaspoon dried oregano leaves
1/8 teaspoon crushed red pepper
1 clove garlic, minced
2 tablespoons grated Parmesan cheese
2 cups shredded mozzarella cheese (8 oz.)

1. Heat oven to 425°F. Spray 13 x 9-inch pan with cooking spray. Unroll dough; place in pan. Starting at center, press out dough in bottom and 1/2 inch up sides of pan to form crust.

2. Bake 7 minutes. Meanwhile, in 8-inch skillet, cook sausage over medium-high heat, stirring frequently, until no longer pink. Remove sausage from skillet; drain on paper towels.

3. In same skillet, mix tomatoes, oregano, red pepper and garlic; cook over medium-high heat until bubbly. Reduce heat to medium-low; simmer uncovered 5 to 8 minutes, stirring occasionally, to blend flavors.

4. Spread tomato mixture over partially baked crust. Sprinkle sausage evenly over tomato mixture. Top with Parmesan and mozzarella cheeses.

5. Return to oven; bake 10 to 12 minutes longer or until cheese is melted and crust is golden brown. Cut into squares.

1 Serving: Calories 300 (Calories from Fat 120); Total Fat 13g (Saturated Fat 6g; Trans Fat 0g); Cholesterol 35mg; Sodium 850mg; Total Carbohydrate 29g (Dietary Fiber 1g; Sugars 6g); Protein 17g
% Daily Value: Vitamin A 6%; Vitamin C 6%; Calcium 25%; Iron 10%
Exchanges: 2 Starch, 1 1/2 Medium-Fat Meat, 1/2 Fat
Carbohydrate Choices: 2

pizza parlor
supreme

start to finish **/ 25 MINUTES**

4 servings

1/4 lb. bulk light turkey and pork sausage
1 medium onion, chopped (1/2 cup)
1/4 cup chopped green bell pepper
1/4 teaspoon fennel seed, crushed, if desired
1/8 to 1/4 teaspoon crushed red pepper
1 package (8 oz.) sliced fresh mushrooms (3 cups)
1 package (10 oz.) prebaked thin Italian pizza crust (12 inch)
1/2 cup pizza sauce
1/2 cup finely shredded mozzarella cheese (2 oz.)
1 tablespoon grated Parmesan cheese

1. Heat oven to 475°F. Heat 10-inch nonstick skillet over medium heat. Add sausage, onion, bell pepper, fennel, if desired, and red pepper; cook 3 to 5 minutes, stirring frequently, until sausage is browned. Add mushrooms; cook 6 minutes, stirring occasionally, just until mushrooms are tender and sausage is no longer pink.

2. Meanwhile, place pizza crust on ungreased cookie sheet. Spoon pizza sauce evenly over crust.

3. Arrange sausage mixture over sauce; sprinkle with mozzarella cheese.

4. Bake 5 to 8 minutes or until cheese is melted. Remove from oven; sprinkle with Parmesan cheese. Cut into wedges.

1 Serving: Calories 370 (Calories from Fat 130); Total Fat 14g (Saturated Fat 6g; Trans Fat 0g); Cholesterol 35mg; Sodium 800mg; Total Carbohydrate 42g (Dietary Fiber 3g; Sugars 5g); Protein 19g
% Daily Value: Vitamin A 10%; Vitamin C 15%; Calcium 15%; Iron 20%
Exchanges: 3 Starch, 1 1/2 Medium-Fat Meat, 1/2 Fat
Carbohydrate Choices: 3

deviled egg and ham salad sandwiches

start to finish **/ 40 MINUTES**

6 sandwiches

6 eggs
1 1/2 cups cubed (1/4 inch) 97%-fat-free hickory-smoked ham (7.5 oz.)
1/2 medium green bell pepper, finely chopped (1/2 cup)
1/4 cup finely chopped red onion
1/3 cup fat-free mayonnaise
1/4 teaspoon ground red pepper (cayenne)
1 tablespoon cider vinegar
1 1/2 teaspoons prepared yellow mustard
6 large leaves lettuce
6 large whole grain sandwich buns, split
6 medium tomatoes, sliced

1. In 2-quart saucepan, place eggs in single layer. Add enough water to cover eggs by 1 inch. Heat to boiling. Immediately remove from heat; cover and let stand 15 minutes. Drain; rinse with cold water. Place eggs in bowl of ice water; let stand 10 minutes.

2. Meanwhile, in medium bowl, mix ham, bell pepper, onion, mayonnaise, ground red pepper, vinegar and mustard until well blended; set aside.

3. Drain water from eggs; peel eggs. Remove egg yolks from egg whites; place yolks in small bowl. Mash yolks; stir into ham mixture. Chop egg whites; stir into ham mixture.

4. Place lettuce on bottom halves of buns. Top each evenly with ham mixture and tomato slices. Cover with top halves of buns.

1 Sandwich: Calories 270 (Calories from Fat: 90); Total Fat 10g (Saturated Fat 3g; Trans Fat 0g); Cholesterol 230mg; Sodium 850mg; Total Carbohydrate 30g (Dietary Fiber 5g; Sugars 10g) Protein 19g
% Daily Value: Vitamin A 25%; Vitamin C 60%; Calcium 8%; Iron 20%
Exchanges: 2 Starch, 2 Lean Meat
Carbohydrate Choices: 1 1/2

colorful veggie and tortilla dinner

4 servings

"We love meat but are really trying to cut down on the amount we eat. We try to make a meatless dinner at least once a week to reduce fat and calories."
—Rich

3/4 cup water

3/4 cup uncooked instant brown rice

2 cups frozen mixed vegetables (from 1-lb. bag), thawed

2 cans (14.5 oz. each) no-salt-added stewed tomatoes, drained

1 can (15.5 oz.) dark red kidney beans, drained, rinsed

1/4 cup finely chopped fresh cilantro

1/2 medium onion, finely chopped (1/4 cup)

1 teaspoon ground cumin

1 teaspoon ground coriander

2 large cloves garlic, minced

1/4 teaspoon pepper

4 fat-free flour tortillas (8 inch), heated

1/2 cup fat-free sour cream

Chopped fresh cilantro

2 medium roma (plum) tomatoes, chopped (2/3 cup)

1. In 2-quart saucepan, heat water to boiling. Stir in rice; return to boiling. Reduce heat; cover and cook 5 to 10 minutes or until liquid is absorbed.

2. Stir in thawed vegetables, stewed tomatoes, beans, 1/4 cup cilantro, the onion, cumin, coriander, garlic and pepper. Cook until thoroughly heated.

3. Place warm tortillas on individual plates. Cover tortillas evenly with rice mixture. Top each with sour cream, chopped cilantro and tomatoes.

1 Serving: Calories 510 (Calories from Fat 15); Total Fat 2g (Saturated Fat 0g; Trans Fat 0g); Cholesterol 0mg; Sodium 600mg; Total Carbohydrate 106g (Dietary Fiber 17g; Sugars 17g); Protein 23g
% Daily Value: Vitamin A 100%; Vitamin C 25%; Calcium 25%; Iron 40%
Exchanges: 5 Starch, 1 Other Carbohydrate, 3 Vegetable
Carbohydrate Choices: 6

colorful veggie and tortilla dinner

linguine and veggies in
parmesan sauce

4 servings (1 1/2 cups each)

> *"I look for recipes that are cooked in one dish because the cleanup is quick. Saving cleanup time is valuable, too."*
> —Carlon

8 oz. uncooked linguine

2 cups fresh broccoli florets

1 cup fresh cauliflower florets

1 cup fresh sugar snap peas, trimmed

1 medium red bell pepper, cut into bite-size strips

2/3 cup shredded Parmesan cheese (2 2/3 oz.)

1/2 cup reduced-fat sour cream

1/4 cup fat-free (skim) milk

1/2 teaspoon salt

1. In Dutch oven, heat 2 quarts (8 cups) water to boiling. Add linguine; cook 5 minutes.

2. Add broccoli and cauliflower; return to boiling. Cook 4 minutes. Add sugar snap peas and bell pepper; cook 2 minutes longer or until linguine is desired doneness and vegetables are crisp-tender.

3. Meanwhile, in small bowl, mix 1/2 cup of the Parmesan cheese, the sour cream, milk and salt until well blended; set aside.

4. Drain linguine and vegetables; place in large serving bowl. Add sour cream mixture; toss gently to mix. If desired, season to taste with pepper and additional salt. Sprinkle with remaining Parmesan cheese.

1 Serving: Calories 360 (Calories from Fat 70); Total Fat 8g (Saturated Fat 4.5g; Trans Fat 0g); Cholesterol 25mg; Sodium 660mg; Total Carbohydrate 57g (Dietary Fiber 7g; Sugars 9g); Protein 19g
% Daily Value: Vitamin A 50%; Vitamin C 100%; Calcium 35%; Iron 20%
Exchanges: 3 Starch, 2 Vegetable, 1 Medium-Fat Meat
Carbohydrate Choices: 3

spinach, shrimp and pasta salad

start to finish **/ 25 MINUTES**

4 servings (1 1/3 cup each)

4 oz. (1 1/2 cups) uncooked rotini (spiral pasta)
3/4 lb. cooked peeled deveined medium shrimp
3 cups torn fresh spinach
1 cup halved cherry tomatoes
1/4 cup purchased fat-free creamy Parmesan salad dressing
3 tablespoons coarsely chopped fresh basil

1. Cook rotini to desired doneness as directed on package. Drain; rinse with cold water to cool.

2. In large bowl, combine cooked rotini, shrimp, spinach and tomatoes. Pour salad dressing over salad; toss gently to coat. Sprinkle with basil.

1 Serving: Calories 220 (Calories from Fat 15); Total Fat 1.5g (Saturated Fat 0g; Trans Fat 0g); Cholesterol 165mg; Sodium 470mg; Total Carbohydrate 30g (Dietary Fiber 4g); Protein 23g
% Daily Value: Vitamin A 60%; Vitamin C 30%; Calcium 6%; Iron 25%
Exchanges: 1 1/2 Starch, 1 Vegetable, 2 1/2 Very Lean Meat
Carbohydrate Choices: 2

5-ingredient dinners

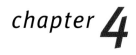

"I never have time to plan dinner ahead, so I really need recipes that use ingredients I have on hand."

—Kelly T.

SUPER EXPRESS *Ready in 20 minutes or less*

italian toast toppers SUPER EXPRESS

start to finish / **15 MINUTES**

8 sandwiches

3/4 lb. lean ground turkey

1 jar (28 oz.) tomato pasta sauce

8 slices Italian bread

8 teaspoons grated Parmesan cheese

1/2 cup shredded mozzarella cheese (2 oz.)

1. Set oven control to broil. In 8-inch skillet, cook ground turkey over medium heat, stirring frequently, until no longer pink; drain. Stir in pasta sauce. Cook, stirring occasionally, until thoroughly heated.

2. Meanwhile, place slices of bread on ungreased cookie sheet. Broil 4 to 6 inches from heat 30 to 60 seconds or until lightly toasted.

3. Turn bread slices over; top each with 1 teaspoon Parmesan cheese. Broil 1 to 1 1/2 minutes or until top is golden brown.

4. Remove from broiler. Spoon turkey mixture evenly onto bread. Top each with mozzarella cheese. Return to broiler; broil 30 to 60 seconds longer or until cheese is melted.

1 Sandwich: Calories 250 (Calories from Fat 80); Total Fat 9g (Saturated Fat 2.5g; Trans Fat 0g); Cholesterol 35mg; Sodium 710mg; Total Carbohydrate 29g (Dietary Fiber 2g; Sugars 7g); Protein 15g
% Daily Value: Vitamin A 15%; Vitamin C 10%; Calcium 10%; Iron 10%
Exchanges: 1 1/2 Starch, 1/2 Other Carbohydrate, 1 1/2 Medium-Fat Meat
Carbohydrate Choices: 2

miniature
ham and swiss
sandwiches SUPER EXPRESS

start to finish / **20 MINUTES**

4 servings (2 sandwiches each)

"I like to try something new to keep my family interested. Raspberry jam and onion rings on a ham and cheese sandwich sounds unusual, but my kids actually liked it!"
—Katie

16 diagonal slices French bread (1/2 inch thick)
1/3 cup raspberry jam
4 oz. thinly sliced cooked extra-lean ham
4 oz. sliced reduced-fat Swiss cheese
1/3 cup thinly sliced red onion, separated into rings

1. Toast bread slices. Spread 1 teaspoon jam on 1 side of each slice.

2. Top 8 slices of bread, jam side up, with ham, cheese and onion rings. Cover with remaining slices of bread, jam side down.

1 Serving: Calories 340 (Calories from Fat 50); Total Fat 5g (Saturated Fat 2g; Trans Fat 0.5g); Cholesterol 25mg; Sodium 820mg; Total Carbohydrate 55g (Dietary Fiber 2g; Sugars 16g); Protein 20g
% Daily Value: Vitamin A 0%; Vitamin C 2%; Calcium 35%; Iron 15%
Exchanges: 2 1/2 Starch, 1 Other Carbohydrate, 2 Very Lean Meat, 1/2 Fat
Carbohydrate Choices: 3 1/2

onion-smothered barbecued turkey burgers SUPER EXPRESS

start to finish **/ 20 MINUTES**

4 sandwiches

1 lb. lean ground turkey
2 tablespoons Italian-style dry bread crumbs
1/3 cup barbecue sauce
1 large sweet or yellow onion
4 whole wheat burger buns or kaiser rolls, split, lightly toasted if desired

1. Set oven control to broil. In medium bowl, mix ground turkey, bread crumbs and half of the barbecue sauce. Shape mixture into 4 patties, 1/2 inch thick. Place patties on rack in broiler pan.

2. Broil 4 to 6 inches from heat 10 to 12 minutes, turning once, until no longer pink and thermometer inserted in center of patties reads 165°F.

3. Meanwhile, halve onion lengthwise; cut crosswise into 1/4-inch-thick slices. Separate into half-rings.

4. Heat 10-inch nonstick skillet over medium-high heat. Add onion; cook 2 minutes, stirring frequently. Reduce heat to medium; cover and cook 2 minutes. Stir in remaining barbecue sauce. Reduce heat to medium-low; cover and cook 5 minutes longer or until onion is wilted and sauce thickens.

5. Place patties on bottom halves of buns. Top with onion mixture. Cover with top halves of buns. If desired, serve with additional barbecue sauce.

1 Sandwich: Calories 300 (Calories from Fat 70); Total Fat 8g (Saturated Fat 2g; Trans Fat 0g); Cholesterol 75mg; Sodium 500mg; Total Carbohydrate 30g (Dietary Fiber 3g; Sugars 11g); Protein 29g
% Daily Value: Vitamin A 2%; Vitamin C 2%; Calcium 6%; Iron 15%
Exchanges: 1 Starch, 1 Other Carbohydrate, 3 1/2 Very Lean Meat, 1 Fat
Carbohydrate Choices: 2

onion-smothered barbecued turkey burgers

hummus
pita pizzas SUPER EXPRESS

start to finish / **15 MINUTES**

4 pizzas

1 can (15 oz.) garbanzo beans, drained, rinsed
4 pita breads (6 to 8 inch)
1 cup finely shredded Parmesan cheese (4 oz.)
Chopped fresh parsley, if desired

1. Set oven control to broil. Line cookie sheet with foil; spray foil with cooking spray. In food processor, process beans until smooth.

2. Spread beans evenly over each pita bread. Sprinkle each with 1/4 cup cheese. Place on cookie sheet.

3. Broil 4 to 6 inches from heat 2 to 4 minutes or until cheese is melted and edges of bread are crisp. Remove from cookie sheet; cut into quarters. If desired, garnish with chopped fresh parsley.

1 Pizza: Calories 400 (Calories from Fat 90); Total Fat 10g (Saturated Fat 5g; Trans Fat 0g); Cholesterol 20mg; Sodium 780mg; Total Carbohydrate 60g (Dietary Fiber 8g; Sugars 3g); Protein 24g
% Daily Value: Vitamin A 4%; Vitamin C 0%; Calcium 45%; Iron 25%
Exchanges: 4 Starch, 1 1/2 Very Lean Meat, 1 Fat
Carbohydrate Choices: 3 1/2

"I don't have a food processor, so I just use my blender to blend these beans. I added a little water, about 3 tablespoons, blended the beans until smooth, and it worked beautifully."
—Cheri

three-cheese
tortilla calzones SUPER EXPRESS

4 calzones

"We're trying to cut down on fat and calories, so we eat meat less often than we used to. My kids won't even miss the meat in this great-tasting sandwich."

—Kelly

1/2 cup reduced-fat ricotta cheese
2 tablespoons grated Parmesan cheese
1/2 cup chunky pizza sauce
4 flour tortillas (10 inch)
1 cup shredded mozzarella cheese (4 oz.)

1. Heat oven to 350°F. In small bowl, mix ricotta and Parmesan cheeses. Spoon 2 tablespoons pizza sauce onto each tortilla; spread evenly to within 1/4 inch of edge.

2. Top half of each tortilla with 1/4 of ricotta mixture and 1/4 of mozzarella cheese. Fold tortillas over filling, pressing edges to seal; place on ungreased cookie sheet.

3. Bake 8 to 10 minutes or until cheese is melted.

1 Calzone: Calories 290 (Calories from Fat 110); Total Fat 12g (Saturated Fat 6g; Trans Fat 0.5g); Cholesterol 25mg; Sodium 590mg; Total Carbohydrate 29g (Dietary Fiber 1g; Sugars 2g); Protein 16g
% Daily Value: Vitamin A 8%; Vitamin C 6%; Calcium 40%; Iron 10%
Exchanges: 2 Starch, 1 1/2 Medium-Fat Meat, 1/2 Fat
Carbohydrate Choices: 2

spicy mexican cheese chowder SUPER EXPRESS

3 servings (1 1/2 cups each)

"It's sometimes hard to predict what my kids will like. But it's good to know that I can turn down the heat by using cheese without the peppers in this quick and hearty chowder."

—Penne

1 can (14 oz.) fat-free chicken broth with 1/3 less sodium
1 bag (1 lb.) frozen broccoli, carrots and cauliflower
1 cup fat-free (skim) milk
2 tablespoons cornstarch
4 oz. Mexican prepared cheese food with jalapeño peppers
    (from 16-oz. loaf), cubed

1. In 3-quart saucepan, heat broth to boiling over high heat. Stir in frozen vegetables. Return to boiling. Reduce heat; cover and simmer 5 minutes.

2. Meanwhile, in small bowl, mix milk and cornstarch until smooth.

3. Stir cornstarch mixture into vegetable mixture, cooking and stirring until thickened. Remove from heat. Stir in cheese until melted. If desired, sprinkle with freshly ground black pepper.

1 Serving: Calories 200 (Calories from Fat 70); Total Fat 8g (Saturated Fat 5g; Trans Fat 0g); Cholesterol 25mg; Sodium 820mg; Total Carbohydrate 20g (Dietary Fiber 4g; Sugars 9g); Protein 14g
% Daily Value: Vitamin A 90%; Vitamin C 40%; Calcium 35%; Iron 8%
Exchanges: 1/2 Starch, 2 Vegetable, 1 High-Fat Meat
Carbohydrate Choices: 1

spicy mexican cheese chowder

chili-stuffed
potatoes

start to finish / **25 MINUTES**

4 servings

"I never decide ahead of time what I'm going to make for dinner, so I stock lots of foods in my pantry. That way I can make a really quick meal without having to to stop to pick something up on my way home. This stuffed potato is perfect for last-minute dinners."

—Nancy

4 medium russet potatoes

1 box or can (14.3 or 15 oz.) fat-free vegetarian chili

1 cup shredded reduced-fat Cheddar cheese or Cheddar–Monterey Jack cheese blend (4 oz.)

Chopped fresh cilantro, if desired

1. Scrub potatoes. Pierce potatoes with fork; arrange in circle on paper towel in microwave. Microwave on High 14 to 16 minutes, rearranging once, until tender. Let stand 5 minutes.

2. Meanwhile, in 1-quart saucepan, heat chili until hot.

3. To serve, split potatoes open; place on individual serving plates. Fluff potatoes with fork. Spoon 1/3 cup chili over each potato. Top each with cheese. If desired, garnish with chopped fresh cilantro.

1 Serving: Calories 240 (Calories from Fat 25); Total Fat 2.5g (Saturated Fat 1.5g; Trans Fat 0g); Cholesterol 5mg; Sodium 590mg; Total Carbohydrate 42g (Dietary Fiber 8g; Sugars 4g); Protein 14g
% Daily Value: Vitamin A 15%; Vitamin C 15%; Calcium 25%; Iron 20%
Exchanges: 3 Starch, 1/2 Very Lean Meat
Carbohydrate Choices: 2

pizza soup SUPER EXPRESS

4 servings (1 1/4 cups each)

1/2 lb. lean ground turkey
2 cloves garlic, minced
1 can (10.75 oz.) condensed reduced-fat tomato soup
1 1/2 cups water
1 cup pizza sauce
1/2 teaspoon sugar
1/4 cup pizza-flavored fish-shaped crackers

1. In 2-quart nonstick saucepan, cook ground turkey and garlic over medium-high heat, stirring frequently, until turkey is no longer pink.

2. Stir in soup, water, pizza sauce and sugar. Heat to boiling. Reduce heat; simmer uncovered 5 minutes or until thoroughly heated. Top individual servings with crackers.

---

1 Serving: Calories 200 (Calories from Fat 70); Total Fat 8g (Saturated Fat 1.5g; Trans Fat 0g); Cholesterol 40mg; Sodium 780mg; Total Carbohydrate 19g (Dietary Fiber 2g, Sugars 8g); Protein 15g
% Daily Value: Vitamin A 10%; Vitamin C 20%; Calcium 4%; Iron 8%
Exchanges: 1 Starch, 1/2 Other Carbohydrate, 1 1/2 Very Lean Meat, 1 Fat
Carbohydrate Choices: 1

black bean
chowder

start to finish / 30 MINUTES

4 servings (1 1/2 cups each)

1 cup cubed (1/2 inch) 97%-fat-free cooked ham
1 medium onion, chopped (1/2 cup)
2 cans (15 oz. each) black beans, drained and rinsed
1 can (14.5 oz.) no-salt-added whole tomatoes, undrained, cut up
1 teaspoon chili powder
Tortilla chips, if desired

1. In 3-quart nonstick saucepan, cook ham and onion over medium heat 4 to 6 minutes, stirring occasionally, until onion is tender.

2. Stir in remaining ingredients. Heat to boiling. Reduce heat to medium-low; simmer uncovered 20 minutes or until slightly thickened. If desired, garnish each serving with a few crushed baked tortilla chips.

1 Serving: Calories 340 (Calories from Fat 30); Total Fat 3g (Saturated Fat 1g; Trans Fat 0g); Cholesterol 20mg; Sodium 440mg; Total Carbohydrate 61g (Dietary Fiber 14g; Sugars 12g); Protein 26g
% Daily Value: Vitamin A 10%; Vitamin C 10%; Calcium 20%; Iron 35%
Exchanges: 2 1/2 Starch, 1 Other Carbohydrate, 1 Vegetable, 2 Very Lean Meat
Carbohydrate Choices: 3

126 *pillsbury good for you!*

citrus
chicken salad SUPER EXPRESS

start to finish **/ 10 MINUTES**

4 servings (2 cups each)

"*This is a very easy, low-fat dinner. I would serve it with whole wheat dinner rolls or breadsticks. We don't often have dessert, but after a light dinner, we might have frozen yogurt with caramel topping.*"
— *Heidi*

6 cups torn romaine
1 can (15 oz.) mandarin orange segments, drained
1 can (10 oz.) 98%-fat-free chicken breast chunks in water, drained
1/3 cup fat-free poppy seed dressing
Fresh mint leaves, if desired

1. In large bowl, gently toss lettuce, orange segments and chicken.

2. Drizzle dressing over salad. If desired, garnish with fresh mint leaves.

1 Serving: Calories 150 (Calories from Fat 10); Total Fat 1.5g (Saturated Fat 0g; Trans Fat 0g); Cholesterol 25mg; Sodium 380mg; Total Carbohydrate 19g (Dietary Fiber 3g; Sugars 13g); Protein 17g
% Daily Value: Vitamin A 60%; Vitamin C 90%; Calcium 4%; Iron 8%
Exchanges: 1 Other Carbohydrate, 2 1/2 Very Lean Meat
Carbohydrate Choices: 1

chicken ravioli
primavera

start to finish / **15 MINUTES**

6 servings (1 cup each)

"I keep quick-cooking ravioli in the freezer for last-minute dinners. It can be stored in the freezer for up to 8 months, so it's convenient to keep on hand."

—Sally

1 package (25 oz.) frozen chicken- or cheese-filled ravioli
3 to 4 small zucchini, halved lengthwise, sliced
1 jar (26 oz.) marinara or tomato pasta sauce
Romano cheese, if desired

1. Cook and drain ravioli as directed on package. Arrange on serving platter or return to saucepan; cover to keep warm.

2. Meanwhile, in 3-quart saucepan, mix zucchini and marinara sauce. Cook over medium-high heat 6 to 7 minutes, stirring occasionally, until zucchini is crisp-tender and sauce is thoroughly heated.

3. Spoon zucchini mixture over cooked ravioli, or add zucchini mixture to ravioli and toss gently. If desired, garnish with grated or shredded Romano cheese.

1 Serving: Calories 360 (Calories from Fat 70); Total Fat 8g (Saturated Fat 1.5g; Trans Fat 0g); Cholesterol 15mg; Sodium 860mg; Total Carbohydrate 61g (Dietary Fiber 4g; Sugars 12g); Protein 14g
% Daily Value: Vitamin A 25%; Vitamin C 20%; Calcium 4%; Iron 15%
Exchanges: 2 Starch, 1 1/2 Other Carbohydrate, 1 Vegetable, 1 High-Fat Meat
Carbohydrate Choices: 4

apricot chicken over COUSCOUS SUPER EXPRESS

start to finish / **20 MINUTES**

4 servings

4 boneless, skinless chicken breasts (1 lb.)
3/4 cup apricot or pineapple preserves
1 box (5.7 oz.) roasted garlic and
olive oil–flavored couscous
1 1/4 cups water
Grated orange peel, if desired

1. Set oven control to broil. Line broiler pan without rack with foil; spray foil with cooking spray. Place chicken in pan. Brush tops of chicken with preserves.

2. Broil 4 to 6 inches from heat 10 to 12 minutes, turning once and brushing frequently with remaining preserves, until juice of chicken is no longer pink when center of thickest part is cut (170°F).

3. Meanwhile, cook couscous in water as directed on box, omitting oil.

4. Spoon couscous onto serving platter; arrange chicken over couscous. If desired, garnish with grated orange peel.

1 Serving: Calories 440 (Calories from Fat 35); Total Fat 4g (Saturated Fat 1g; Trans Fat 0g); Cholesterol 70mg; Sodium 85mg; Total Carbohydrate 73g (Dietary Fiber 3g; Sugars 30g); Protein 30g
% Daily Value: Vitamin A 0%; Vitamin C 4%; Calcium 4%; Iron 8%
Exchanges: 3 Starch, 2 Other Carbohydrate, 3 Very Lean Meat
Carbohydrate Choices: 5

lemon-basil
skillet chicken
with rice SUPER EXPRESS

4 servings

"I try to save time wherever I can. If I use a mallet or rolling pin to pound the chicken breasts in this recipe to an even thickness, I can shave off about 5 minutes of cooking time."

—Liz

4 boneless, skinless chicken breasts (1 lb.)
Paprika
1 1/2 cups hot water
1 1/2 cups uncooked instant white rice
2 tablespoons butter or margarine
1 tablespoon lemon juice
1 teaspoon dried basil leaves
1/4 teaspoon salt

1. Heat 10-inch nonstick skillet over high heat. Sprinkle both sides of chicken breasts with paprika; add to hot skillet. Immediately reduce heat to medium-high; cover and cook 4 minutes.

2. Meanwhile, in 2-quart saucepan, place hot water; cover tightly. Heat to boiling. Stir in rice; remove from heat. Let stand 5 minutes.

3. Turn chicken; cover and cook 4 to 5 minutes longer or until juice of chicken is no longer pink when center of thickest part is cut (170°F). Remove chicken from skillet; place on serving platter. Cover to keep warm.

4. In same hot skillet, mix butter, lemon juice, basil and salt. If necessary, return to heat to melt butter.

5. Place rice on serving platter; arrange chicken over rice. Spoon butter mixture over chicken.

1 Serving: Calories 340 (Calories from Fat 90); Total Fat 10g (Saturated Fat 4g; Trans Fat 0g); Cholesterol 85mg; Sodium 250mg; Total Carbohydrate 35g (Dietary Fiber 0g; Sugars 0g); Protein 28g
% Daily Value: Vitamin A 6%; Vitamin C 0%; Calcium 4%; Iron 15%
Exchanges: 2 Starch, 3 Very Lean Meat, 1 1/2 Fat
Carbohydrate Choices: 2

lemon-basil skillet chicken with rice

pork and noodle
primavera SUPER EXPRESS

start to finish **/ 20 MINUTES**

4 servings (1 cup each)

"I love to make one-pot meals; it really saves cleanup time. And because lean chops and tenderloin are very lean, I feel good about serving them to my family."

—Libby

2 boneless pork loin chops (1/2 lb.) or 1/2 lb. pork tenderloin, cut into thin bite-size strips
2 cups water
2 packages (3 oz. each) oriental-flavor ramen noodle soup mix
1/4 teaspoon ground ginger
1 cup ready-to-eat baby-cut carrots
1 cup fresh sugar snap peas, trimmed

1. Heat 10-inch nonstick skillet over medium-high heat. Add pork; cook and stir until lightly browned.

2. Stir in water, contents of seasoning packets from both soup mixes, ginger and carrots. Heat to boiling. Reduce heat to low; cover and simmer 3 minutes or until carrots are crisp-tender.

3. Gently break noodles; add to skillet with sugar snap peas. Heat to boiling, separating noodles with fork and stirring into liquid as they soften. Reduce heat to medium; cover and cook 2 to 3 minutes or until sugar snap peas are tender.

1 Serving: Calories 290 (Calories from Fat 120); Total Fat 13g (Saturated Fat 4g; Trans Fat 2.5g); Cholesterol 35mg; Sodium 740mg; Total Carbohydrate 30g (Dietary Fiber 3g; Sugars 3g); Protein 17g
% Daily Value: Vitamin A 120%; Vitamin C 10%; Calcium 2%; Iron 10%
Exchanges: 1 1/2 Starch, 1 Vegetable, 1 1/2 Lean Meat, 1 1/2 Fat
Carbohydrate Choices: 2

snacks to pack

You're in luck! This chapter contains more than great on-the-go dinners. Here are a few easily totable, nutritious snacks to make your life easier too.

savory snack mix

Prep: 20 min; Cool: 15 min

> 3/4 cup each toasted whole-grain oat cereal, bite-size squares crisp corn cereal, oyster crackers, cheese-flavored tiny fish-shaped crackers and broken pretzel sticks
> 4 teaspoons soy sauce
> 1 1/2 teaspoons Dijon mustard
> 3/4 teaspoon each garlic and onion powder

1 Heat oven to 350°F. Spray 15 x 10 x 1-inch pan with cooking spray. In large bowl, mix both cereals, both crackers and the pretzel sticks.

2 In small bowl, mix remaining ingredients until well blended. Drizzle over cereal mixture; toss to coat evenly. Spread mixture evenly in pan.

3 Bake 5 minutes. Stir; bake 3 to 5 minutes longer. Cool completely, about 15 minutes. Store in tightly covered container or resealable plastic food-storage bags.

6 servings (1/2 cup each)

blueberry-popcorn bars

Prep: 25 min

> 1 bag (3.5 oz.) butter-flavor microwave popcorn with 50% less fat than regular microwave popcorn or 12 cups air-popped popcorn
> 1 package (3.5 oz.) dried blueberries (1/2 to 2/3 cup)
> 1 bag (10.5 oz.) miniature marshmallows
> 1/2 cup white vanilla chips
> 1 tablespoon butter or margarine

1 Spray 13 x 9-inch pan and large bowl with cooking spray. If using microwave popcorn, pop as directed on bag. In bowl, mix popcorn and dried blueberries; set aside.

2 In medium microwavable bowl, place marshmallows, vanilla chips and butter. Microwave on High 1 minute. Stir mixture; microwave on High 1 to 3 minutes longer, stirring occasionally, until marshmallows and chips can be stirred smooth.

3 Pour marshmallow mixture over popcorn mixture; stir until evenly coated (mixture will be sticky). Pour into pan. Spray hands or large rubber spatula with cooking spray. Press popcorn mixture in pan. Place in freezer until set, no longer than 10 minutes.

4 With serrated knife, cut into bars. Store in tightly covered container or wrap each bar in foil or plastic wrap.

16 bars

blueberry-popcorn bars

cranberry-cinnamon trail mix

Prep: 5 min

> 2 1/2 cups bite-size squares crisp wheat, rice and corn bran cereal
> 1 1/2 cups sweetened whole-grain oat cereal with apple and cinnamon
> 2 packages (3.5 oz. each) sweetened dried cranberries (2 cups)
> 1/2 cup white vanilla chips

In 2-quart container with cover or half-gallon resealable plastic food-storage bag, mix all ingredients. Cover container tightly or seal bag. If desired, divide mixture into small resealable plastic food-storage bags for packing.

12 servings (1/2 cup each)

couscous-stuffed
red bell peppers SUPER EXPRESS

start to finish / **20 MINUTES**

2 servings (2 pepper halves each)

"I'm always looking for quick and easy recipes served in a different way. And I love the peppers in this recipe because I don't have to precook them, plus they're so fresh tasting."

—Mary

1 box (5.7 oz.) roasted garlic and olive oil–flavored couscous
1 1/4 cups water
2 large red bell peppers, cut in half lengthwise, seeds and membranes removed
1 cup chopped fresh spinach
1/4 cup grated Parmesan cheese

1. Cook couscous in water as directed on box, omitting oil; cover to keep warm.

2. Meanwhile, in 8-inch square (2-quart) microwavable dish, arrange bell pepper halves; add 2 tablespoons water. Cover with microwavable waxed paper. Microwave on High 3 to 4 minutes or just until crisp-tender.

3. Stir spinach and cheese into couscous. Spoon mixture into pepper halves.

1 Serving: Calories 390 (Calories from Fat 40); Total Fat 4.5g (Saturated Fat 2.5g; Trans Fat 0g); Cholesterol 10mg; Sodium 260mg; Total Carbohydrate 74g (Dietary Fiber 8g; Sugars 12g); Protein 17g
% Daily Value: Vitamin A 220%; Vitamin C 260%; Calcium 20%; Iron 10%
Exchanges: 4 1/2 Starch, 1 Vegetable, 1/2 Fat
Carbohydrate Choices: 4 1/2

couscous-stuffed red bell peppers

country breaded
pork chops

start to finish / **35 MINUTES**

4 servings

1/2 cup corn flake crumbs
1 tablespoon Dijon mustard
2 teaspoons orange juice
1/4 teaspoon dried thyme leaves
4 boneless pork loin chops, 3/4 inch thick (1 lb.)

1. Heat oven to 425°F. Line cookie sheet with foil; spray foil lightly with cooking spray. In shallow dish, place corn flake crumbs. In small bowl, mix mustard, orange juice and thyme.

2. Brush 1 side of each pork chop with mustard mixture. Place 1 chop, mustard side down, in crumbs; brush remaining side of chop with mustard mixture. Turn chop to coat both sides well with crumbs. Place on cookie sheet. Repeat with remaining chops.

3. Bake 20 to 25 minutes or until pork is no longer pink and thermometer inserted in center of pork reads 160°F.

1 Serving: Calories 200 (Calories from Fat 80); Total Fat 9g (Saturated Fat 3g; Trans Fat 0g); Cholesterol 70mg; Sodium 190mg; Total Carbohydrate 7g (Dietary Fiber 0g; Sugars 0g); Protein 25g
% Daily Value: Vitamin A 2%; Vitamin C 2%; Calcium 0%; Iron 15%
Exchanges: 1/2 Starch, 3 Lean Meat
Carbohydrate Choices: 1/2

apricot-glazed
lamb chops

8 servings

> *"I am always looking for easy and new recipes to serve to my family. This one is extra-quick; I'll pick a really fast side dish like couscous or pasta to go with it."*
>
> —Becky

1/4 cup apricot preserves or jam, large pieces finely chopped
2 teaspoons chopped fresh tarragon or 1/2 teaspoon dried tarragon leaves
1/4 teaspoon Dijon mustard
8 lean lamb rib chops (about 1 1/4 lb.)
1/4 teaspoon salt
1/8 teaspoon pepper

1. Heat oven to 450°F. Line 15 x 10-inch pan with sides with foil. In small bowl, mix preserves, tarragon and mustard; set aside.

2. Heat 10-inch nonstick skillet over medium-high heat. Sprinkle both sides of lamb chops with salt and pepper; place in hot skillet. Cook 4 to 6 minutes, turning once, until brown on both sides. Place lamb in pan; spoon apricot mixture evenly over tops.

3. Bake 7 to 10 minutes or until desired doneness.

1 Serving: Calories 200 (Calories from Fat 90); Total Fat 10g (Saturated Fat 3.5g; Trans Fat 1g); Cholesterol 70mg; Sodium 140mg; Total Carbohydrate 7g (Dietary Fiber 0g; Sugars 5g); Protein 20g
% Daily Value: Vitamin A 0%; Vitamin C 0%; Calcium 0%; Iron 8%
Exchanges: 1/2 Other Carbohydrate, 3 Lean Meat
Carbohydrate Choices: 1/2

pork lo mein SUPER EXPRESS

start to finish / **15 MINUTES**

4 servings (1 3/4 cups each)

"I take shortcuts in the kitchen. When I need to thaw frozen vegetables, I place them in a colander and rinse them with warm water. Then I make sure they're well drained before I add them to the quick-cooking pasta."

—Kathy

4 oz. uncooked capellini (angel hair) pasta
1 pork tenderloin (3/4 lb.)
1 bag (1 lb.) frozen broccoli, carrots and cauliflower, thawed
1/2 cup teriyaki baste and glaze
1/4 teaspoon ground ginger

1. Cook pasta as directed on package, omitting salt. Drain; cover to keep warm.

2. Meanwhile, cut pork tenderloin in half lengthwise; cut crosswise into 1/4-inch-thick slices.

3. Heat 10-inch nonstick skillet over medium-high heat. Add pork; cook and stir 3 minutes. Stir in frozen vegetables, teriyaki baste and glaze, and ginger. Heat to boiling. Reduce heat to medium-low; cover and simmer 3 to 5 minutes, stirring once, until pork is no longer pink in center and vegetables are crisp-tender.

4. Gently stir in cooked pasta. Cook until thoroughly heated.

1 Serving: Calories 240 (Calories from Fat 40); Total Fat 4.5g (Saturated Fat 1.5g; Trans Fat 0g); *Cholesterol* 80mg; Sodium 760mg; Total Carbohydrate 27g (Dietary Fiber 4g; Sugars 4g); Protein 26g
% Daily Value: Vitamin A 60%; Vitamin C 30%; Calcium 4%; Iron 15%
Exchanges: 1 1/2 Starch, 1 Vegetable, 2 1/2 Very Lean Meat, 1/2 Fat
Carbohydrate Choices: 2

spiced apple
pork chops

start to finish **/ 20 MINUTES**

4 servings

"*I need more time-saving recipes like this one. This easy recipe would be great served with any pasta, rice or stuffing—or even coleslaw made with reduced-fat dressing.*"

—*Tina*

4 boneless pork loin chops, 3/4 inch thick (1 lb.)
1/2 teaspoon pumpkin pie spice
1/4 teaspoon salt
1/8 teaspoon pepper
1 tablespoon apple or crabapple jelly, melted

1. Set oven control to broil. Line broiler pan without rack with foil; spray foil with cooking spray. Sprinkle both sides of pork chops with pumpkin pie spice, salt and pepper; place in pan.

2. Broil 4 to 6 inches from heat 7 to 10 minutes, turning once, until pork is no longer pink and thermometer inserted in center of pork reads 160°F. Brush pork with melted jelly; broil 30 to 60 seconds longer to glaze.

1 Serving: Calories 190 (Calories from Fat 80); Total Fat 9g (Saturated Fat 3g; Trans Fat 0g); Cholesterol 70mg; Sodium 190mg; Total Carbohydrate 3g (Dietary Fiber 0g; Sugars 2g); Protein 24g
% Daily Value: Vitamin A 0%; Vitamin C 0%; Calcium 0%; Iron 6%
Exchanges: 3 1/2 Lean Meat
Carbohydrate Choices: 0

pan-roasted halibut
over rotini SUPER EXPRESS

start to finish / **15 MINUTES**

4 servings

2 2/3 cups uncooked rainbow rotini pasta (8 oz.)
4 halibut fillets, 1/2 to 3/4 inch thick (4 oz. each), skin removed
1 teaspoon seasoned salt
1/2 teaspoon coarse ground black pepper

1. Cook pasta as directed on package. Drain; cover to keep warm.

2. Meanwhile, sprinkle both sides of halibut with salt and pepper. Heat 10-inch nonstick skillet over high heat. Immediately place fish in skillet; cook 1 minute or until golden brown.

3. Turn fish; reduce heat to medium. Add 1/3 cup water; cover and cook 5 to 8 minutes or until fish flakes easily with fork. Serve fish over pasta.

1 Serving: Calories 310 (Calories from Fat 20); Total Fat 2.5g (Saturated Fat 0g; Trans Fat 0g); Cholesterol 60mg; Sodium 660mg; Total Carbohydrate 45g (Dietary Fiber 3g; Sugars 0g); Protein 29g
% Daily Value: Vitamin A 0%; Vitamin C 0%; Calcium 2%; Iron 15%
Exchanges: 3 Starch, 3 Very Lean Meat
Carbohydrate Choices: 3

pan-roasted halibut over rotini

fish
provençal SUPER EXPRESS

start to finish / **15 MINUTES**

4 servings

4 thin green bell pepper rings
4 slices tomato (1/2 inch thick)
4 slices red onion (1/4 inch thick)
3/4 lb. tilapia fillets (1/4 to 1/2 inch thick), cut into 4 pieces
1/2 teaspoon dried basil leaves
Cooking spray

1. Set oven control to broil. Line 15 x 10-inch pan with sides with foil; spray foil lightly with cooking spray. Place bell pepper rings in pan. Top each with tomato and onion slice.

2. Place tilapia pieces next to vegetable stacks in pan. Sprinkle fish and vegetables with basil; spray lightly with cooking spray.

3. Broil 4 to 6 inches from heat 5 to 8 minutes or until fish flakes easily with fork. Serve fish with vegetable stacks.

1 Serving: Calories 100 (Calories from Fat 15); Total Fat 1.5g (Saturated Fat 0g; Trans Fat 0g); Cholesterol 45mg; Sodium 75mg; Total Carbohydrate 5g (Dietary Fiber 1g; Sugars 3g); Protein 17g
% Daily Value: Vitamin A 6%; Vitamin C 15%; Calcium 2%; Iron 2%
Exchanges: 1 Vegetable, 2 Very Lean Meat
Carbohydrate Choices: 0

simple honey-glazed
salmon and rice

start to finish **/ 30 MINUTES**

4 servings

"What could be simpler than this easy recipe? It's just what I'm looking for—the ketchup and honey are surprisingly good with the salmon. And it's so good for all of us to eat more fish."

—Cheri

Salmon
1 sockeye or Atlantic salmon fillet (1 lb.), cut into 4 pieces
1 tablespoon honey
1 tablespoon ketchup

Rice
1 cup uncooked instant brown rice
1 1/4 cups water

1. Heat oven to 450°F. Line cookie sheet with foil; spray foil with cooking spray. Place salmon on cookie sheet. In small bowl, mix honey and ketchup. Spread over fish.

2. Bake 12 to 18 minutes or until fish flakes easily with fork.

3. Meanwhile, cook rice in water as directed on package. Serve fish with rice.

1 Serving: Calories 310 (Calories from Fat 90); Total Fat 10g (Saturated Fat 1.5g; Trans Fat 0g); Cholesterol 75mg; Sodium 115mg; Total Carbohydrate 28g (Dietary Fiber 2g; Sugars 5g); Protein 26g
% Daily Value: Vitamin A 4%; Vitamin C 0%; Calcium 0%; Iron 4%
Exchanges: 2 Starch, 3 Lean Meat
Carbohydrate Choices: 2

tomato and cheese
pasta skillet

start to finish **/ 30 MINUTES**

4 servings (1 cup each)

1 can (15 oz.) Italian-style tomato sauce
1 3/4 cups water
1 package (7 oz.) small pasta shells (2 cups)
2 tablespoons finely chopped onion
3/4 cup shredded mozzarella cheese (3 oz.)

1. In 8-inch skillet, mix tomato sauce, water, pasta and onion. Heat to boiling. Reduce heat to medium-low; cover and simmer 12 minutes, stirring occasionally.

2. Sprinkle cheese over top. Cover; cook 1 minute longer or until cheese is melted.

1 Serving: Calories 360 (Calories from Fat 80); Total Fat 9g (Saturated Fat 3.5g; Trans Fat 0g); Cholesterol 10mg; Sodium 640mg; Total Carbohydrate 60g (Dietary Fiber 4g, Sugars 9g); Protein 13g
% Daily Value: Vitamin A 15%; Vitamin C 15%; Calcium 20%; Iron 15%
Exchanges: 4 Starch, 1 Fat
Carbohydrate Choices: 4

tomato and cheese pasta skillet

one-dish
pasta *SUPER EXPRESS*

start to finish **/ 20 MINUTES**

2 servings (1 1/2 cups each)

1/4 lb. fresh green beans, cut into 2-inch pieces (1 cup)
1 cup fat-free (skim) milk
1 package (4.8 oz.) angel hair pasta mix with herb sauce
1/2 cup cubed cooked lean roast beef (3 oz.)

1. In Dutch oven or 3-quart nonstick saucepan, heat 1 1/3 cups water to boiling. Add green beans. Reduce heat to medium-low; cover and simmer 5 minutes.

2. Gradually stir milk and contents of herb packet from pasta mix into green beans. Heat to boiling over high heat. Stir in pasta; return to boiling, stirring frequently (if necessary, separate pasta with fork). Reduce heat to medium; cook uncovered 4 to 5 minutes, stirring frequently, until pasta is tender.

3. Stir in roast beef. Cook, stirring occasionally, until thoroughly heated.

1 Serving: Calories 260 (Calories from Fat 80); Total Fat 9g (Saturated Fat 3.5g; Trans Fat 0g); Cholesterol 40mg; Sodium 390mg; Total Carbohydrate 26g (Dietary Fiber 3g; Sugars 10g); Protein 20g
% Daily Value: Vitamin A 15%; Vitamin C 2%; Calcium 25%; Iron 15%
Exchanges: 1 Starch, 1/2 Other Carbohydrate, 1 Vegetable, 2 Very Lean Meat, 1 1/2 Fat
Carbohydrate Choices: 2

chicken packets
milano

4 servings

"Fresh sage adds a mellow flavor that ground sage just can't match— that's why I grow it in my home herb garden."
—Kristi

4 boneless, skinless chicken breasts (1 lb.)
1/4 cup reduced-calorie zesty Italian or Italian Parmesan dressing
4 slices tomato
12 fresh sage leaves or 1/2 teaspoon ground sage

1. Heat oven to 450°F. Cut 4 (12 x 12-inch) sheets of heavy-duty foil. Place 1 chicken breast in center of each. Top each with 1 tablespoon dressing, 1 slice of tomato and 3 sage leaves.

2. Wrap each packet securely using double-fold seals, allowing room for heat expansion. Place packets on ungreased cookie sheet.

3. Bake 20 to 25 minutes or until juice of chicken is no longer pink when centers of thickest pieces are cut and thermometer inserted in center reads 165°F. Carefully open packets to allow steam to escape.

1 Serving: Calories 160 (Calories from Fat 60); Total Fat 6g (Saturated Fat 1.5g; Trans Fat 0g); Cholesterol 70mg; Sodium 260mg; Total Carbohydrate 2g (Dietary Fiber 0g; Sugars 1g); Protein 25g
% Daily Value: Vitamin A 4%; Vitamin C 4%; Calcium 0%; Iron 6%
Exchanges: 3 1/2 Very Lean Meat, 1 Fat
Carbohydrate Choices: 0

on-the-go dinners

"*Because we spend so much time on the way to the kids' events, our dinners are often eaten on the go. Having a healthy dinner to eat in the car would be a dream come true.*"

—*Cheri O.*

SUPER EXPRESS *Ready in 20 minutes or less*

roast beef
panini SUPER EXPRESS

start to finish / **15 MINUTES**

4 servings

1 package (10 oz.) ready-to-serve Italian pizza crusts (two 6-inch crusts)
4 tablespoons light garlic-and-herb spreadable cheese (from 4- to 6.5-oz. container)
1 cup spinach leaves
1/4 lb. thinly sliced 97%-fat-free cooked Italian roast beef (from deli)
1 large tomato, sliced
1/4 cup sliced ripe olives
2 tablespoons shredded Parmesan cheese

1. Spread top side of 1 pizza crust and bottom side of other pizza crust with spreadable cheese.

2. On crust with top spread with cheese, layer remaining ingredients. Top with second crust, cheese side down. Cut into 8 wedges. Wrap 2 wedges together securely with foil or plastic wrap; take with you for an on-the-go dinner.

1 Serving: Calories 320 (Calories from Fat 120); Total Fat 13g (Saturated Fat 6g; Trans Fat 0g); Cholesterol 45mg; Sodium 590mg; Total Carbohydrate 35g (Dietary Fiber 3g; Sugars 2g); Protein 19g
% Daily Value: Vitamin A 25%; Vitamin C 20%; Calcium 10%; Iron 20%
Exchanges: 2 1/2 Starch, 1 1/2 Very Lean Meat, 2 Fat
Carbohydrate Choices: 2

roast beef panini

teriyaki beef pocket
sandwiches *SUPER EXPRESS*

start to finish / **20 MINUTES**

4 servings (2 sandwiches each)

1 lb. boneless beef sirloin steak (1 inch thick), cut into thin bite-size strips
1/4 teaspoon garlic powder
1/4 cup teriyaki baste and glaze
4 pita breads (6 inch), cut in half to form pockets
2 medium tomatoes, sliced
8 small leaves lettuce

1. In small bowl, mix beef strips, garlic powder and 1 tablespoon of the teriyaki baste and glaze.

2. Heat 10-inch nonstick skillet over medium-high heat. Add beef mixture; cook 4 to 6 minutes, stirring frequently, until beef is browned and desired doneness. Stir in remaining baste and glaze; cook until thoroughly heated.

3. Fill each pita bread half evenly with tomato slices, lettuce and beef mixture. Wrap 2 sandwiches together securely with foil; take with you for an on-the-go dinner.

---

1 Serving: Calories 310 (Calories from Fat 40); Total Fat 4.5g (Saturated Fat 1.5g; Trans Fat 0g); Cholesterol 60mg; Sodium 890mg; Total Carbohydrate 39g (Dietary Fiber 2g; Sugars 3g); Protein 30g
% Daily Value: Vitamin A 10%; Vitamin C 10%; Calcium 6%; Iron 25%
Exchanges: 2 Starch, 1 Vegetable, 3 Very Lean Meat, 1/2 Fat
Carbohydrate Choices: 2 1/2

bbq beef
tortillas

start to finish / **25 MINUTES**

4 sandwiches

"My kids absolutely love the taste of barbecue—they could eat it almost every night. This recipe is quick, easy and something the whole family enjoys."

—Renee

1/2 lb. beef sirloin steak, cut into thin bite-size strips
1 cup frozen whole kernel corn (from 1-lb. bag)
1/2 cup barbecue sauce
4 flour tortillas (8 inch), heated
1 large tomato, chopped (1 cup)
1/4 cup shredded reduced-fat Cheddar cheese (1 oz.)

1. Heat 8-inch nonstick skillet over medium-high heat. Add beef; cook 4 to 6 minutes, stirring frequently, until browned.

2. Stir in corn and barbecue sauce. Reduce heat to medium; cover and cook 5 minutes, stirring occasionally, until hot.

3. Place warm tortillas on individual plates. Spoon beef mixture evenly down center of each tortilla. Top each with tomato and cheese. Fold tortillas in half or roll up. Wrap each sandwich securely with foil; take with you for an on-the-go dinner.

1 Sandwich: Calories 300 (Calories from Fat 50); Total Fat 6g (Saturated Fat 1.5g; Trans Fat 0.5g); Cholesterol 30mg; Sodium 610mg; Total Carbohydrate 45g (Dietary Fiber 3g; Sugars 10g); Protein 18g
% Daily Value: Vitamin A 10%; Vitamin C 10%; Calcium 10%; Iron 15%
Exchanges: 2 Starch, 1 Other Carbohydrate, 1 1/2 Very Lean Meat, 1 Fat
Carbohydrate Choices: 3

beef and cabbage
wraps SUPER EXPRESS

start to finish / **15 MINUTES**

6 wraps

"When sweet
summer onions
are no longer
available, I
substitute red
onions. The
milder-flavored
onions have a
short storage life,
so avoid buying
any that have
begun to sprout
or have soft
spots."

—Jackie

3/4 lb. beef sirloin strips for stir-fry
1 medium sweet onion, chopped
3 cups coleslaw mix (shredded cabbage and carrots)
1/3 cup barbecue sauce
6 flour tortillas (8 to 10 inch), heated

1. Heat 10-inch nonstick skillet over medium-high heat. Add beef and onion; cook 3 minutes, stirring frequently, until browned.

2. Reduce heat to medium. Gently stir in coleslaw mix. Cover; cook about 2 minutes, stirring once, until cabbage is slightly wilted. Remove from heat. Stir in barbecue sauce.

3. Spoon mixture evenly onto center of each warm tortilla. To roll each, fold 1 end of tortilla up over filling; fold right and left sides over folded end, overlapping edges. Roll up tightly. Wrap each wrap securely with foil; take with you for an on-the-go dinner.

1 Wrap: Calories 230 (Calories from Fat 45); Total Fat 5g (Saturated Fat 1.5g; Trans Fat 0.5g); Cholesterol 30mg; Sodium 370mg; Total Carbohydrate 33g (Dietary Fiber 2g; Sugars 6g); Protein 16g
% Daily Value: Vitamin A 20%; Vitamin C 10%; Calcium 8%; Iron 15%
Exchanges: 2 Starch, 1 Vegetable, 1 Lean Meat
Carbohydrate Choices: 2

beef and cabbage wraps

ham and vegetable
tortilla rolls

start to finish **/ 25 MINUTES**

4 roll-ups

4 flour tortillas (8 to 10 inch)

4 tablespoons reduced-fat garden vegetable cream cheese spread
(from 8-oz. container)

1 package (6 oz.) thinly sliced 97%-fat-free cooked ham

1 cup shredded lettuce

8 thin slices tomato

1 small cucumber, cut into thin strips

1/2 green bell pepper, cut into thin strips

1/2 cup shredded mozzarella or smoked provolone cheese (2 oz.)

1. Spread each tortilla evenly with 1 tablespoon cream cheese spread. Top evenly with remaining ingredients.

2. Roll up tortillas. Cut each diagonally in half; secure with toothpicks. Wrap each roll-up securely with foil or plastic wrap; take with you for an on-the-go dinner.

1 Roll-Up: Calories 280 (Calories from Fat 90); Total Fat 10g (Saturated Fat 4.5g; Trans Fat 0.5g); Cholesterol 40mg; Sodium 780mg; Total Carbohydrate 30g (Dietary Fiber 2g; Sugars 4g); Protein 18g
% Daily Value: Vitamin A 15%; Vitamin C 20%; Calcium 20%; Iron 15%
Exchanges: 1 1/2 Starch, 1 Vegetable, 1 1/2 Very Lean Meat, 1 1/2 Fat
Carbohydrate Choices: 2

chicken and couscous
roll-ups SUPER EXPRESS

start to finish / **15 MINUTES**

6 roll-ups

"I was so excited to see this recipe. My kids love couscous, and I try to think of different ways to serve it. We also like whole wheat tortillas, so I keep them to increase the number of grains we eat."
—Cheri

1 box (5.7 oz.) roasted garlic and olive oil-flavored couscous
1 1/4 cups water
1 tablespoon olive or canola oil
1 can (10 oz.) chunk chicken in water, drained
6 flour tortillas (8 inch)
6 tablespoons reduced-fat sour cream
1/2 cup chopped tomato (1 small)
1/4 cup chopped fresh cilantro

1. Cook couscous as directed on box using water and oil.

2. Stir in chicken. Spoon about 1/2 cup couscous mixture onto each tortilla. Top each with sour cream, tomato and cilantro. Roll up. Wrap each roll-up securely with foil or plastic wrap; take with you for an on-the-go dinner.

1 Roll-Up: Calories 330 (Calories from Fat 40); Total Fat 4.5g (Saturated Fat 1g; Trans Fat 0g); Cholesterol 25mg; Sodium 630mg; Total Carbohydrate 57g (Dietary Fiber 5g; Sugars 3g); Protein 17g
% Daily Value: Vitamin A 6%; Vitamin C 6%; Calcium 10%; Iron 15%
Exchanges: 4 Starch, 1 Very Lean Meat
Carbohydrate Choices: 3 1/2

chicken and apple "clams" *SUPER EXPRESS*

start to finish / **15 MINUTES**

6 sandwiches

> "We've started to cut down on fat by combining ingredients that work well together. Mayonnaise has a lot of fat and yogurt doesn't, so a recipe made with both will be lower in fat and still have great taste. The family won't even know the difference."
>
> —Kevin

3 tablespoons mayonnaise or salad dressing
3 tablespoons plain fat-free yogurt
1/8 teaspoon seasoned salt
1 cup chopped cooked chicken breast
1 medium tart-sweet red apple, cored, cut into bite-size pieces (about 3/4 cup)
3 tablespoons thinly sliced celery
6 whole wheat or white mini pita breads

1. In medium bowl, mix mayonnaise, yogurt and seasoned salt. Gently stir in chicken, apple and celery to coat.

2. Cut slit in side of each pita bread to open and form pocket. Fill each with 1/3 cup chicken mixture. Wrap each sandwich securely with foil or plastic wrap; take with you for an on-the-go dinner.

1 Sandwich: Calories 170 (Calories from Fat 20); Total Fat 2.5g (Saturated Fat 0.5g; Trans Fat 0g); Cholesterol 20mg; Sodium 350mg; Total Carbohydrate 29g (Dietary Fiber 4g; Sugars 6g); Protein 12g
% Daily Value: Vitamin A 0%; Vitamin C 2%; Calcium 2%; Iron 10%
Exchanges: 2 Starch, 1 Very Lean Meat
Carbohydrate Choices: 2

158 *pillsbury good for you!*

chicken and apple "clams"

speedy chicken
fajita wraps

start to finish / **20 MINUTES**

4 wraps

> "These wraps make a tasty supper that my husband and I enjoy and my kids love. And it's faster than going out for fast food."
> — Sharon

4 fat-free flour tortillas (8 inch)

3 packages (4 oz. each) marinated mesquite barbecue-flavored chicken breast fillets, cut into thin strips

1 medium green bell pepper, cut into thin bite-size strips

1 teaspoon chili powder

2 tablespoons water

1/2 cup shredded Cheddar cheese (2 oz.)

1/4 cup fat-free sour cream

1. Heat tortillas as directed on package; keep warm.

2. Meanwhile, heat 10-inch nonstick skillet over medium-high heat. Add chicken; cook and stir 1 minute. Stir in bell pepper and chili powder. Add water; cover and cook 2 to 3 minutes, stirring occasionally, until chicken is no longer pink in center and bell pepper is crisp-tender.

3. Spoon chicken mixture evenly onto warm tortillas. Top each with 2 tablespoons cheese and 1 tablespoon sour cream. Fold in 3 sides of each tortilla to enclose filling. Wrap each wrap securely with foil; take with you for an on-the-go dinner.

1 Wrap: Calories 350 (Calories from Fat 130); Total Fat 15g (Saturated Fat 6g; Trans Fat 0.5g); Cholesterol 60mg; Sodium 860mg; Total Carbohydrate 30g (Dietary Fiber 2g; Sugars 3g); Protein 25g
% Daily Value: Vitamin A 10%; Vitamin C 20%; Calcium 15%; Iron 10%
Exchanges: 2 Starch, 2 1/2 Very Lean Meat, 2 1/2 Fat
Carbohydrate Choices: 2

chicken pita
taquitos SUPER EXPRESS

start to finish / **20 MINUTES**

4 servings (2 sandwiches each)

"This is a really fun sandwich and is very easy to make with flavored chicken strips. If there are ingredients that our family doesn't like or I don't have on hand like the chili or the cilantro, I just leave them out."

—Susan

1 package (8.25 oz.) frozen fajita-style cooked chicken strips

1 small zucchini, cut in half lengthwise, sliced

1 small onion, sliced

1/2 medium green bell pepper, thinly sliced

1 cup frozen whole kernel corn (from 1-lb. bag)

1 large tomato, chopped (1 cup)

1/2 jalapeño chili, seeded, finely chopped

1 tablespoon chopped fresh cilantro

4 whole wheat pita breads (6 inch), cut in half to form pockets

1. Cook chicken as directed on package in microwave until juice of chicken is no longer pink when center of thickest part is cut (170°F).

2. Meanwhile, heat 10-inch nonstick skillet over medium-high heat. Add zucchini, onion and bell pepper; cook 4 minutes, stirring frequently. Stir in corn, tomato, chili pepper and cilantro. Reduce heat to medium-low; simmer uncovered 3 minutes or until vegetables are tender and mixture is thoroughly heated.

3. Thinly slice cooked chicken; stir into vegetable mixture. Fill each pita bread half with about 2/3 cup chicken and vegetable mixture. Wrap 2 sandwiches together securely with foil; take with you for an on-the-go dinner.

---

1 Serving: Calories 340 (Calories from Fat 60); Total Fat 7g (Saturated Fat 2g; Trans Fat 0g); Cholesterol 60mg; Sodium 800mg; Total Carbohydrate 49g (Dietary Fiber 7g; Sugars 9g); Protein 26g
% Daily Value: Vitamin A 15%; Vitamin C 25%; Calcium 2%; Iron 15%
Exchanges: 3 Starch, 1 Vegetable, 2 Very Lean Meat, 1/2 Fat
Carbohydrate Choices: 3

crispy cabbage and chicken wraps SUPER EXPRESS

start to finish / **10 MINUTES**

4 wraps

3/4 lb. chicken or turkey breast strips for stir-fry

1 bag (16 oz.) coleslaw mix (shredded cabbage and carrots)

1/2 teaspoon caraway seed, crushed

3 tablespoons mustard-mayonnaise sauce or fat-free mayonnaise

4 flour tortillas (10 inch), heated

1. Heat 10-inch nonstick skillet over medium-high heat. Add chicken; cook and stir 3 minutes or until no longer pink in center.

2. Stir in coleslaw mix and caraway seed. Reduce heat to medium; cover and cook 3 minutes or just until cabbage wilts, but remains crisp. Remove from heat. Stir in mustard-mayonnaise sauce until well mixed.

3. Spoon mixture evenly down center of each warm tortilla. Fold sides of each tortilla over filling; roll up. Wrap each wrap securely with foil; take with you for an on-the-go dinner.

1 Wrap: Calories 350 (Calories from Fat 70); Total Fat 8g (Saturated Fat 2g; Trans Fat 1g); Cholesterol 50mg; Sodium 550mg; Total Carbohydrate 47g (Dietary Fiber 4g; Sugars 5g); Protein 26g
% Daily Value: Vitamin A 110%; Vitamin C 25%; Calcium 15%; Iron 20%
Exchanges: 3 Starch, 1 Vegetable, 2 Lean Meat
Carbohydrate Choices: 3

mediterranean chicken sandwiches SUPER EXPRESS

start to finish **/ 15 MINUTES**

4 sandwiches

"This is such a quick-to-make sandwich. If I get a chance, I make the dressing ahead of time to give it a stronger herb flavor."

—Phyllis

Dressing
3 tablespoons reduced-fat mayonnaise or salad dressing
1/2 teaspoon dried oregano leaves
1/4 teaspoon dry ground mustard
1/4 teaspoon dried basil leaves
1 small clove garlic, minced

Sandwiches
8 slices multigrain bread
1 cup fresh spinach leaves
1 package (6 oz.) sliced cooked chicken breast
1/2 medium cucumber, cut into 20 thin slices
4 thin slices red onion

1. In small bowl, mix dressing ingredients until well blended. Spread about 1 teaspoon dressing on each slice of bread.

2. Top 4 slices of bread evenly with spinach, chicken, cucumber and onion. Cover each with second slice of bread, dressing side down. Wrap each sandwich securely with foil or plastic wrap; take with you for an on-the-go dinner.

1 Sandwich: Calories 240 (Calories from Fat 70); Total Fat 8g (Saturated Fat 1.5g; Trans Fat 0g); Cholesterol 40mg; Sodium 390mg; Total Carbohydrate 27g (Dietary Fiber 4g; Sugars 7g); Protein 19g
% Daily Value: Vitamin A 15%; Vitamin C 8%; Calcium 6%; Iron 15%
Exchanges: 1 1/2 Starch, 1 Vegetable, 1 1/2 Very Lean Meat, 1 Fat
Carbohydrate Choices: 2

turkey
poorboy
sandwiches SUPER EXPRESS

start to finish **/ 10 MINUTES**

4 sandwiches

1 medium carrot, shredded (3/4 cup)

1/4 cup raisins

1/2 cup vanilla fat-free yogurt

3 tablespoons fat-free mayonnaise or salad dressing

4 French rolls (2 oz. each), halved lengthwise

1/2 lb. thinly sliced cooked lean turkey breast

4 leaves leaf lettuce

1. In small bowl, mix carrots, raisins, yogurt and mayonnaise.

2. Spread cut sides of both halves of each roll with carrot mixture. Fill each roll with turkey and lettuce leaf. Wrap each sandwich securely with foil or plastic wrap; take with you for an on-the-go dinner.

1 Sandwich: Calories 300 (Calories from Fat 30); Total Fat 3g (Saturated Fat 1g; Trans Fat 0g); Cholesterol 50mg; Sodium 480mg; Total Carbohydrate 45g (Dietary Fiber 3g; Sugars 13g); Protein 24g
% Daily Value: Vitamin A 80%; Vitamin C 10%; Calcium 10%; Iron 15%
Exchanges: 2 Starch, 1 Other Carbohydrate, 2 1/2 Very Lean Meat
Carbohydrate Choices: 3

dine-in
desserts

Dining in tonight? Make it extra-fun for everyone by serving one of these super-simple desserts. And here's another tip—get the kids to help!

lemon-raspberry parfaits

Prep: 15 min

> 1 pint (2 cups) vanilla fat-free ice cream
> 1/4 cup lemon curd (from a jar) or lemon pie filling (from 15.75-oz. can)
> 2 tablespoons lemon juice
> 1 1/4 cups frozen (thawed) fat-free whipped topping
> 1 cup fresh or frozen (thawed) unsweetened raspberries

1 Line cookie sheet with waxed paper. With 1-inch diameter ice cream scoop, scoop 24 balls of ice cream onto cookie sheet. Freeze while making lemon mixture.

2 In small bowl, mix lemon curd and lemon juice until smooth. Fold in 1 cup of the whipped topping. Chill until serving time.

3 To serve, place 3 ice cream balls in each of 4 (6-oz.) stemmed parfait glasses. Top with half of lemon mixture and raspberries. Repeat layers. Top each with 1 tablespoon remaining whipped topping. Garnish with lemon peel strips.

4 servings

strawberry-orange fool

Prep: 15 min; Chill: 45 min

> 1/2 cup fat-free sour cream
> 1 tablespoon powdered sugar
> 1 teaspoon grated orange peel
> 1 tablespoon orange-flavored liqueur or orange juice
> 1 1/2 cups frozen (thawed) fat-free whipped topping
> 3 cups sliced fresh strawberries

1 In medium bowl, mix sour cream, powdered sugar, orange peel and liqueur. Fold in whipped topping.

2 For each serving, use 1/3 cup orange cream and 3/4 cup strawberries. In each dessert dish, layer 2 tablespoons cream, half of berries, 2 tablespoons cream, remaining half of berries and remaining cream. Refrigerate until chilled, about 45 minutes or until serving time. Store in refrigerator.

4 servings

star-studded berries

Prep: 20 min; Cool: 10 min

> 1 refrigerated pie crust (from 15-oz. box), softened as directed on box
> 2 teaspoons sugar
> 1/4 teaspoon ground cardamom
> 4 cups mixed fresh berries (such as sliced strawberries, blackberries and/or blueberries)
> 1/4 to 1/3 cup sugar
> 2 tablespoons orange juice

1 Heat oven to 450°F. Line cookie sheet with foil. Remove crust from pouch; place crust flat on work surface. If necessary, press out folds or creases. With 3 1/2-inch star-shaped cookie cutter, cut 9 stars from pie crust; place stars on cookie sheet.

2 In small bowl, mix 2 teaspoons sugar and cardamom. Lightly brush tops of stars with water; sprinkle with sugar mixture.

3 Bake 6 to 8 minutes or until lightly browned. Remove from cookie sheet; cool on wire rack about 10 minutes.

4 Meanwhile, in medium bowl, gently mix berries, 1/4 to 1/3 cup sugar and the orange juice. To serve, divide berry mixture evenly onto dessert plates. Top each with pastry star.

9 servings

strawberry-orange fool

club turkey
wraps SUPER EXPRESS

start to finish **/ 15 MINUTES**

4 wraps

> *"I think of this recipe as an old-fashioned club sandwich turned into a contemporary wrap. The salsa-flavored mayo jazzes up the flavor."*
>
> *—David*

2 slices reduced-sodium bacon, halved
4 flour tortillas (8 to 10 inch)
1/2 cup fat-free mayonnaise
1/2 cup chunky-style salsa
4 large leaves romaine
1 1/2 cups chopped cooked turkey (about 1/2 lb.)

1. In 10-inch nonstick skillet, cook bacon until crisp; drain on paper towels.

2. Meanwhile, heat tortillas as directed on package. In small bowl, mix mayonnaise and salsa.

3. Top each warm tortilla evenly with lettuce, turkey, mayonnaise mixture and bacon. Fold both sides of each tortilla towards center, overlapping slightly; secure each with 2 toothpicks. Cut each in half. Wrap each wrap securely with foil; take with you for an on-the-go dinner.

1 Wrap: Calories 270 (Calories from Fat 80); Total Fat 9g (Saturated Fat 2.5g; Trans Fat 0.5g); Cholesterol 45mg; Sodium 660mg; Total Carbohydrate 30g (Dietary Fiber 2g; Sugars 4g); Protein 18g
% Daily Value: Vitamin A 10%; Vitamin C 15%; Calcium 8%; Iron 15%
Exchanges: 2 Starch, 1 1/2 Lean Meat, 1/2 Fat
Carbohydrate Choices: 2

two-cheese and turkey mexican pizzas

start to finish / **30 MINUTES**

2 pizzas

4 oz. fat-free cream cheese, softened

2 teaspoons lime juice

1 teaspoon ground cumin

2 flour tortillas (8 to 10 inch)

2 oz. sliced smoked turkey breast (from deli), cut into strips

1/2 cup drained canned black beans, rinsed

1/2 cup frozen whole kernel corn (from 1-lb. bag), thawed

1 medium tomato, diced

1/2 cup shredded reduced-fat Monterey Jack or Cheddar cheese (2 oz.)

2 tablespoons chopped fresh cilantro

1. Heat oven to 425°F. Line cookie sheet with foil; spray foil with cooking spray. In small bowl, mix cream cheese, lime juice and cumin until well blended.

2. Spread cream cheese mixture evenly over tortillas. Place on cookie sheet. Top each with turkey, beans, corn, tomato and cheese.

3. Bake 5 minutes or until pizzas are thoroughly heated and cheese is melted. Sprinkle with cilantro; cut into wedges. Wrap each pizza securely with foil; take with you for an on-the-go dinner.

---

1 Pizza: Calories 420 (Calories from Fat 100); Total Fat 11g (Saturated Fat 5g; Trans Fat 0.5g); Cholesterol 50mg; Sodium 780mg; Total Carbohydrate 50g (Dietary Fiber 6g; Sugars 7g); Protein 33g
% Daily Value: Vitamin A 30%; Vitamin C 10%; Calcium 40%; Iron 25%
Exchanges: 3 1/2 Starch, 3 Lean Meat
Carbohydrate Choices: 3

turkey barbecues

start to finish / **30 MINUTES**

6 sandwiches

1 1/2 cups chopped cooked turkey breast (about 1/2 lb.)
3/4 cup barbecue sauce
6 whole wheat burger buns, split, lightly toasted
6 tablespoons shredded Colby-Monterey Jack cheese blend

1. Heat oven to 350°F. In medium bowl, mix turkey and barbecue sauce.

2. Place toasted bottom halves of buns, cut side up, on ungreased cookie sheet. Spread each evenly with turkey mixture. Top each with 1 tablespoon cheese.

3. Bake 15 to 20 minutes or until sandwiches are thoroughly heated and cheese is melted. Cover with toasted top halves of buns. Wrap each sandwich securely with foil; take with you for an on-the-go dinner.

---

1 Sandwich: Calories 210 (Calories from Fat 40); Total Fat 4g (Saturated Fat 2g; Trans Fat 0g); Cholesterol 40mg; Sodium 560mg; Total Carbohydrate 28g (Dietary Fiber 3g; Sugars 12g); Protein 17g
% Daily Value: Vitamin A 2%; Vitamin C 0%; Calcium 10%; Iron 10%
Exchanges: 1 Starch, 1 Other Carbohydrate, 2 Very Lean Meat, 1/2 Fat
Carbohydrate Choices: 2

turkey, ham and cheese
bagel-wiches SUPER EXPRESS

start to finish / **15 MINUTES**

4 sandwiches

2 tablespoons fat-free mayonnaise or salad dressing
1 teaspoon honey mustard
4 multigrain bagels, split, toasted
4 slices (1.5 oz. each) cooked turkey breast
4 slices (1 oz. each) cooked ham
1 slice (1.5 oz.) provolone cheese, cut into quarters
4 thin slices tomato

1. Set oven control to broil. In small bowl, mix mayonnaise and mustard. Place toasted bottom halves of bagels on ungreased cookie sheet. Spread each with mayonnaise mixture. Top each evenly with turkey, ham and cheese.

2. Broil 4 to 6 inches from heat 2 to 3 minutes or until cheese is melted. Top each with tomato slice and toasted top half of bagel. Wrap each sandwich securely with foil; take with you for an on-the-go dinner.

1 Sandwich: Calories 300 (Calories from Fat 50); Total Fat 6g (Saturated Fat 2.5g; Trans Fat 0g); Cholesterol 60mg; Sodium 720mg; Total Carbohydrate 39g (Dietary Fiber 3g; Sugars 6g); Protein 27g
% Daily Value: Vitamin A 4%; Vitamin C 2%; Calcium 10%; Iron 20%
Exchanges: 2 Starch, 1/2 Other Carbohydrate, 3 Very Lean Meat, 1/2 Fat
Carbohydrate Choices: 2 1/2

quick chicken
subs SUPER EXPRESS

start to finish / **15 MINUTES**

4 sandwiches

1/4 cup fat-free mayonnaise or salad dressing
4 hoagie buns (2 oz. each), split
1 1/2 cups shredded lettuce
1/4 lb. thinly sliced 98%-fat-free cooked chicken breast
1 large tomato, cut into 8 slices
2 oz. reduced-fat hot pepper cheese, shredded (1/2 cup)

"I look for ingredients my family will like. We all like everything in this easy chicken sandwich. That makes it much easier for me, the cook for tonight."

— Bob

Spread mayonnaise on cut sides of hoagie buns. Layer remaining ingredients evenly on bottom halves of buns. Top with top halves of buns. Wrap each sandwich securely with foil or plastic wrap; take with you for an on-the-go dinner.

1 Sandwich: Calories 260 (Calories from Fat 60); Total Fat 6g (Saturated Fat 3g; Trans Fat 0g); Cholesterol 35mg; Sodium 590mg; Total Carbohydrate 35g (Dietary Fiber 3g; Sugars 8g); Protein 17g
% Daily Value: Vitamin A 10%; Vitamin C 15%; Calcium 15%; Iron 10%
Exchanges: 2 Starch, 1 Vegetable, 1 Very Lean Meat, 1 Fat
Carbohydrate Choices: 2

turkey and pepper
hoagies SUPER EXPRESS

start to finish / **15 MINUTES**

4 sandwiches

1/2 cup fat-free mayonnaise or salad dressing
1 teaspoon Italian seasoning
1/2 lb. smoked turkey breast slices, cut into strips
2 cups frozen bell pepper and onion stir-fry (from 1-lb. bag)
4 hoagie buns (6 inch), split

1. In small bowl, mix mayonnaise and Italian seasoning; set aside.

2. Heat 10-inch nonstick skillet over medium-high heat. Add turkey and bell pepper and onion stir-fry; cook and stir 1 minute. Cover; cook 2 minutes.

3. Meanwhile, spread about 1 tablespoon mayonnaise mixture on cut sides of buns.

4. Uncover skillet; cook and stir 1 to 3 minutes longer or until liquid evaporates and bell pepper is tender.

5. Spoon turkey mixture evenly onto bottom halves of buns. Cover with top halves of buns. Wrap each sandwich securely with foil; take with you for an on-the-go dinner.

1 Sandwich: Calories 300 (Calories from Fat 35); Total Fat 3.5g (Saturated Fat 1g; Trans Fat 0g); Cholesterol 50mg; Sodium 670mg; Total Carbohydrate 44g (Dietary Fiber 4g; Sugars 9g); Protein 24g
% Daily Value: Vitamin A 4%; Vitamin C 50%; Calcium 8%; Iron 15%
Exchanges: 2 1/2 Starch, 1 Vegetable, 2 Very Lean Meat
Carbohydrate Choices: 3

soft-shell
turkey tacos

4 servings (2 sandwiches each)

"Recipes that are easy with familiar ingredients are most appealing to me. These quick tacos are just that. Forming the tortillas into cone shapes makes them easy to eat on the go."

—Jason

3/4 lb. ground turkey breast
1 teaspoon chili powder
1 can (14.5 oz.) Mexican-style stewed tomatoes, undrained, cut up
8 flour tortillas (7 inch), heated
1/2 cup shredded reduced-fat Monterey Jack cheese (2 oz.)
1 cup shredded lettuce

1. Heat 8-inch nonstick skillet over medium-high heat. Add ground turkey and chili powder; cook 5 to 6 minutes, stirring frequently, until turkey is no longer pink. Stir in tomatoes. Reduce heat to medium; cook 10 minutes, stirring occasionally, until liquid has evaporated.

2. Spoon turkey mixture evenly down center of each tortilla. Top each with cheese and lettuce. Roll tortillas into cone shape. Wrap 2 sandwiches together securely with foil; take with you for an on-the-go dinner.

1 Serving: Calories 400 (Calories from Fat 110); Total Fat 13g (Saturated Fat 4.5g; Trans Fat 1g); Cholesterol 65mg; Sodium 780mg; Total Carbohydrate 45g (Dietary Fiber 3g; Sugars 6g); Protein 29g
% Daily Value: Vitamin A 15%; Vitamin C 10%; Calcium 20%; Iron 20%
Exchanges: 3 Starch, 3 Lean Meat
Carbohydrate Choices: 3

take-along
turkey-vegetable
sandwiches

start to finish **/ 25 MINUTES**

6 sandwiches

1 tablespoon honey

3 tablespoons Dijon mustard

1 cup sliced fresh mushrooms

1/2 cup thinly sliced red onion

1 small red bell pepper, cut into small thin strips

1 small yellow bell pepper, cut into small thin strips

2 tablespoons red wine vinegar

6 tablespoons reduced-fat garden vegetable cream cheese spread
(from 8-oz. container)

1 loaf French bread (1 lb.), cut in half lengthwise

1 package (6 oz.) thinly sliced low-fat oven-roasted turkey breast

1. In small bowl, mix honey and mustard; set aside.

2. Heat 8-inch nonstick skillet over medium heat. Add mushrooms, onion, both bell peppers and vinegar; cook, stirring occasionally, until peppers are crisp-tender.

3. Spread cream cheese spread on cut side of top half of bread. Spread mustard mixture on cut side of bottom half of bread.

4. Arrange half of turkey on bottom half of bread. Top with vegetable mixture and top half of bread. Cut loaf into 6 sandwiches. Wrap each sandwich securely with foil; take with you for an on-the-go dinner.

1 Sandwich: Calories 300 (Calories from Fat 50); Total Fat 6g (Saturated Fat 2g; Trans Fat 0.5g); Cholesterol 30mg; Sodium 730mg; Total Carbohydrate 46g (Dietary Fiber 3g; Sugars 7g); Protein 17g
% Daily Value: Vitamin A 20%; Vitamin C 80%; Calcium 10%; Iron 15%
Exchanges: 3 Starch, 1 Lean Meat
Carbohydrate Choices: 3

crunchy
seafood
sandwiches SUPER EXPRESS

start to finish / 20 MINUTES

4 servings (2 sandwiches each)

"Using prepared ingredients makes cooking (and life) so much easier. Purchased coleslaw mix and frozen cooked shrimp make a super-quick filling for these super-tasty pocket sandwiches."
— *Polly*

6 oz. frozen cooked peeled deveined shrimp, tail shells removed, thawed, drained and coarsely chopped

2 cups coleslaw mix (shredded cabbage and carrots)

1 medium green onion, sliced (1/4 cup)

1/2 cup fat-free mayonnaise or salad dressing

4 whole wheat or white pita breads (6 or 7 inch), cut in half to form pockets

8 leaves red leaf lettuce

4 thin slices tomato, halved

1. In medium bowl, gently mix shrimp, coleslaw mix, onions, mayonnaise, dill and salt.

2. Fill each pita bread half with 1 lettuce leaf, 1 halved tomato slice and 1/4 cup shrimp mixture. Wrap 2 sandwiches together securely with foil or plastic wrap; take with you for an on-the-go dinner.

1 Serving: Calories 250 (Calories from Fat 30); Total Fat 3g (Saturated Fat 1g; Trans Fat 0g); Cholesterol 85mg; Sodium 700mg; Total Carbohydrate 44g (Dietary Fiber 7g; Sugars 10g); Protein 16g
% Daily Value: Vitamin A 110%; Vitamin C 15%; Calcium 6%; Iron 25%
Exchanges: 2 Starch, 1/2 Other Carbohydrate, 1 Vegetable, 1 Very Lean Meat
Carbohydrate Choices: 2 1/2

crunchy seafood sandwiches

ham salad melts SUPER EXPRESS

start to finish **/ 20 MINUTES**

4 servings (1 sandwich each)

1 cup diced cooked ham (about 1/4 lb.)
1/4 cup finely chopped celery
1/4 cup chopped green bell pepper
2 tablespoons finely chopped onion
1/2 cup reduced-calorie mayonnaise or salad dressing
3 drops red pepper sauce
4 slices whole wheat bread, toasted
4 slices (.75 oz. each) fat-free American cheese, each cut into 4 triangles

1. Heat oven to 350°F. In small bowl, mix ham, celery, bell pepper, onion, mayonnaise and red pepper sauce. Spread evenly on toasted bread; place on ungreased cookie sheet.

2. Bake 5 minutes. Slice cheese into triangles. Place 2 cheese triangles on each slice of bread; bake 5 minutes longer. Wrap securely with foil; take with you for an on-the-go dinner.

1 Serving: Calories 200 (Calories from Fat: 80); Total Fat 9g (Saturated Fat 2g; Trans Fat 0g); Cholesterol 25mg; Sodium 920mg; Total Carbohydrate 17g (Dietary Fiber 2g; Sugars 5g); Protein 13g
% Daily Value: Vitamin A 4%; Vitamin C 8%; Calcium 10%; Iron 8%
Exchanges: 1 Starch, 1 1/2 Very Lean Meat, 1 1/2 Fat
Carbohydrate Choices: 1

spicy bean and
rice wraps SUPER EXPRESS

start to finish / **10 MINUTES**

6 wraps

"Cleanup for this recipe is a snap because you heat the beans and cook the instant rice together in one skillet. I look for dinners that cook in one pan so cleanup is easier and quicker, then I have more time to spend with my family."

—Sherri

1 can (15 oz.) spicy chili beans, undrained
3/4 cup uncooked instant rice
1/3 cup water
1 medium bell pepper (any color)
1 medium tomato
6 flour tortillas (8 inch), heated

1. In 10-inch nonstick skillet, mix beans, rice and water. Heat to boiling. Reduce heat to medium-low; cover and cook 5 to 8 minutes or until rice is tender. Meanwhile, chop bell pepper and tomato; set aside.

2. Spoon bean mixture evenly onto center of each warm tortilla. Top each evenly with bell pepper and tomato. To roll each, fold 1 end of tortilla up over filling; fold right and left sides over folded end, overlapping edges. Roll up tightly (if needed, secure with toothpick). Wrap each wrap securely with foil; take with you for an on-the-go dinner.

1 Wrap: Calories 250 (Calories from Fat 30); Total Fat 3.5g (Saturated Fat 1g; Trans Fat 0g); Cholesterol 0mg; Sodium 720mg; Total Carbohydrate 49g (Dietary Fiber 5g; Sugars 2g); Protein 9g
% Daily Value: Vitamin A 10%; Vitamin C 25%; Calcium 8%; Iron 20%
Exchanges: 3 Starch, 1 Vegetable
Carbohydrate Choices: 3

foot-long pizza

start to finish **/ 30 MINUTES**

4 servings

"I've been looking for dinner recipes that are easy, quick to make and healthy. And it's not easy to find them. This one is all those things and is delicious, too!"

—Karen

1 loaf French bread (12 inch), cut in half lengthwise
1/4 cup garlic-and-herb spreadable cheese (from 4 to 6.5-oz. container)
1 cup thinly sliced mushrooms
1 cup thin strips red, green or yellow bell pepper
1/2 cup julienne-cut zucchini (2 x 1/4 x 1/4 inch)
1/3 cup sliced ripe olives
Olive oil flavor or regular cooking spray
1 teaspoon Italian seasoning
1 cup shredded reduced-fat mozzarella cheese (4 oz.)

1. Heat oven to 450°F. Line 15 x 10-inch pan with sides with foil. Place bread halves, cut side up, in pan.

2. Spread spreadable cheese evenly over each bread half. Arrange mushrooms, bell pepper, zucchini and olives evenly over top. Spray gently with cooking spray. Sprinkle with Italian seasoning.

3. Bake 15 minutes or just until vegetables begin to brown. Remove from oven; reduce oven temperature to 425°F. Sprinkle cheese over pizza.

4. Return to oven; bake at 425°F 5 minutes longer or until cheese is melted. Cut each bread half in half crosswise. Wrap each serving securely with foil; take with you for an on-the-go dinner.

1 Serving: Calories 300 (Calories from Fat 120); Total Fat 13g (Saturated Fat 7g; Trans Fat 0.5g); Cholesterol 25mg; Sodium 690mg; Total Carbohydrate 33g (Dietary Fiber 3g; Sugars 2g); Protein 14g
% Daily Value: Vitamin A 35%; Vitamin C 40%; Calcium 30%; Iron 15%
Exchanges: 2 Starch, 1 High-Fat Meat, 1 Fat
Carbohydrate Choices: 2

foot-long pizza

grill it!

chapter 6

"Our family loves grilling and we are always looking for shortcuts. Even 10 minutes makes a big difference when it comes to making dinner."

—Diane C.

SUPER EXPRESS **Ready in 20 minutes or less**

steak and
potato salad

start to finish **/ 30 MINUTES**

4 servings (2 cups each)

"We all love the taste of grilled meat and it goes so well with the veggies in this terrific salad. I didn't think that eating healthy could taste this good."

—Jason

1/2 lb. small new red potatoes, halved
2/3 cup fat-free honey Dijon dressing
3/4 lb. boneless beef sirloin steak (3/4 inch thick)
1/4 teaspoon salt
1/4 teaspoon coarse ground black pepper
4 cups torn romaine
2 medium tomatoes, cut into thin wedges
1/2 cup thinly sliced red onion

1. Heat gas or charcoal grill. In 2-quart saucepan, place potatoes and enough water to cover. Heat to boiling. Reduce heat to medium; cook 5 to 8 minutes or just until potatoes are fork-tender.

2. Drain potatoes; place in medium bowl. Gently stir in 2 tablespoons of the dressing to coat. Brush steak with 1 tablespoon of the remaining dressing; sprinkle with salt and pepper.

3. When grill is heated, place steak and potatoes on gas grill over medium heat or on charcoal grill over medium coals; cover grill. Cook 8 to 15 minutes, turning once, until steak is desired doneness and potatoes are golden brown.

4. Arrange lettuce, tomatoes and onion on large serving platter. Cut steak into thin slices; arrange on platter. Top with potatoes. Drizzle salad with remaining dressing. If desired, sprinkle with additional black pepper.

1 Serving: Calories 210 (Calories from Fat 30); Total Fat 3g (Saturated Fat 1g; Trans Fat 0g); Cholesterol 45mg; Sodium 610mg; Total Carbohydrate 29g (Dietary Fiber 4g; Sugars 10g); Protein 20g
% Daily Value: Vitamin A 35%; Vitamin C 50%; Calcium 4%; Iron 20%
Exchanges: 1 Starch, 1 Other Carbohydrate, 2 1/2 Very Lean Meat
Carbohydrate Choices: 2

chicken-vegetable salad

5 servings (2 cups each)

"It's great to be able to make the whole meal on the grill. This recipe is very quick and uses ingredients I have on hand, a big plus for me."

—Diane

1 1/2 cups uncooked rotini pasta (4 oz.)

4 boneless, skinless chicken breasts (about 1 lb.)

1/2 cup reduced-calorie Caesar dressing with 1/3 less fat

1 medium zucchini, cut lengthwise into 1/2-inch-thick slices

1 medium red bell pepper, halved, seeded

1/2 small eggplant, peeled, cut into 1/2-inch-thick slices

4 cups chopped romaine

1. Heat gas or charcoal grill. Cook pasta as directed on package. Drain; rinse with cold water to cool. Drain well.

2. Meanwhile, brush chicken with 1 tablespoon of the dressing (if desired, sprinkle chicken with salt and pepper).

3. When grill is heated, place chicken, zucchini, bell pepper (skin side down) and eggplant on gas grill over medium heat or on charcoal grill over medium coals; cover grill. Cook 10 to 13 minutes, turning once, until juice of chicken is no longer pink when center of thickest part is cut (170°F) and vegetables are tender.

4. Cut chicken and vegetables into bite-size pieces; place in large bowl. Gently stir in cooked pasta and lettuce. Pour remaining dressing over salad; toss gently to coat.

1 Serving: Calories 250 (Calories from Fat 45); Total Fat 5g (Saturated Fat 1g; Trans Fat 0g); Cholesterol 60mg; Sodium 410mg; Total Carbohydrate 29g (Dietary Fiber 4g; Sugars 7g); Protein 26g
% Daily Value: Vitamin A 50%; Vitamin C 50%; Calcium 4%; Iron 15%
Exchanges: 1 Starch, 1/2 Other Carbohydrate, 1 Vegetable, 3 Very Lean Meat, 1/2 Fat
Carbohydrate Choices: 2

best west
tex-mex burgers

start to finish / **25 MINUTES**

6 sandwiches

"Because we have burgers on the grill so often, I look for different ways to make them. Recipes need to be simple and foods that my 11-year-old and 7-year old will eat. This one fits all of those things."

—Kelly

1/4 cup corn flake crumbs
2/3 cup chunky-style salsa
1 lb. extra-lean (at least 90%) ground beef
3/4 cup fat-free sour cream
2 tablespoons chopped green chiles (from 4.5-oz. can)
1/4 teaspoon ground cumin
6 fat-free flour tortillas (8 to 10 inch)
1 1/2 cups chopped leaf lettuce

1. Heat gas or charcoal grill. In large bowl, mix corn flake crumbs and 3 tablespoons of the salsa. Stir in ground beef. Shape mixture into 6 round or long, narrow (hot dog–shaped) patties, 1/2 inch thick.

2. In small bowl, mix sour cream, green chiles and cumin; set aside.

3. When grill is heated, place patties on gas grill over medium heat or on charcoal grill over medium coals; cover grill. Cook 11 to 13 minutes, turning once, until patties are no longer pink in center and juice is clear and thermometer inserted in center of patties reads 160°F. Just before burgers are done, wrap tortillas in foil; place on grill for 1 minute to heat.

4. To serve, sprinkle 1/4 cup lettuce down center of each tortilla. Top each with patty. Spoon sour cream mixture evenly over patties. Roll up tortillas. Serve with remaining salsa.

1 Sandwich: Calories 320 (Calories from Fat 60); Total Fat 7g (Saturated Fat 2.5g; Trans Fat 0g); Cholesterol 50mg; Sodium 730mg; Total Carbohydrate 42g (Dietary Fiber 4g; Sugars 3g); Protein 22g
% Daily Value: Vitamin A 15%; Vitamin C 6%; Calcium 10%; Iron 25%
Exchanges: 1 1/2 Starch, 1 1/2 Other Carbohydrate, 2 1/2 Very Lean Meat, 1 Fat
Carbohydrate Choices: 3

cajun country
beef burgers

start to finish / **30 MINUTES**

4 sandwiches

1 lb. extra-lean (at least 90%) ground beef
1/4 cup finely chopped celery
1/2 medium onion, finely chopped (1/4 cup)
1/4 cup finely chopped green bell pepper
2 teaspoons Cajun seasoning or 1/4 to 1/2 teaspoon ground red pepper (cayenne)
8 diagonal slices French bread (3/4 inch thick)
1 1/2 cups chopped curly endive (chicory) or dandelion greens
1/4 cup mesquite or hickory smoke-flavored barbecue sauce

1. Heat gas or charcoal grill. In large bowl, mix ground beef, celery, onion, bell pepper and Cajun seasoning. Shape mixture into 4 flat oval-shaped patties, 1/2 inch thick.

2. When grill is heated, place patties on gas grill over medium heat or on charcoal grill over medium coals; cover grill. Cook 11 to 13 minutes, turning once, until patties are no longer pink in center and juice is clear and thermometer inserted in center of patties reads 160°F.

3. To serve, top 4 slices of bread with endive and patties. Spoon 1 tablespoon barbecue sauce on each patty. Cover with remaining bread slices.

1 Sandwich: Calories 290 (Calories from Fat 90); Total Fat 10g (Saturated Fat 4g; Trans Fat 1g); Cholesterol 70mg; Sodium 690mg; Total Carbohydrate 26g (Dietary Fiber 2g; Sugars 5g); Protein 25g
% Daily Value: Vitamin A 6%; Vitamin C 10%; Calcium 6%; Iron 20%
Exchanges: 1 Starch, 1/2 Other Carbohydrate, 3 Lean Meat
Carbohydrate Choices: 2

new england open-faced
turkey burgers

start to finish / **25 MINUTES**

6 sandwiches

2 cups herb-flavored stuffing mix (4 oz.)

1/3 cup fat-free chicken broth with 1/3 less sodium (from 14-oz. can)

1 lb. lean ground turkey

6 slices New England–style raisin brown bread, 3/4 inch thick (from 1-lb. can) or
　　3 plain or onion buns, split

1 can (8 oz.) whole berry cranberry sauce

6 leaves romaine

1. Heat gas or charcoal grill. In large bowl, mix stuffing mix and half of the broth. Stir in remaining broth until well mixed. Add turkey; mix well. Shape mixture into 6 flat oval-shaped patties, 1/2 inch thick.

2. When grill is heated, place patties on gas grill over medium-high heat or on charcoal grill over medium-high coals; cover grill. Cook 14 to 16 minutes, turning once, until patties are no longer pink and thermometer inserted in center of patties reads 165°F.

3. To serve, spread 1 side of each slice of bread with 1 to 2 teaspoons cranberry sauce. Top with lettuce leaves, patties and remaining cranberry sauce.

1 Sandwich: Calories 350 (Calories from Fat 80); Total Fat 9g (Saturated Fat 2.5g; Trans Fat 0g); Cholesterol 50mg; Sodium 670mg; Total Carbohydrate 49g (Dietary Fiber 4g; Sugars 18g); Protein 20g
% Daily Value: Vitamin A 8%; Vitamin C 4%; Calcium 6%; Iron 15%
Exchanges: 2 1/2 Starch, 1 Other Carbohydrate, 2 Lean Meat
Carbohydrate Choices: 3

terrific
turkey burgers SUPER EXPRESS

6 sandwiches

"I always keep lean ground beef in the freezer, but I don't always have ground turkey. I know I can substitute one for the other in this terrific-tasting burger."
—Jeanne

1 lb. ground turkey breast or lean ground turkey
1/2 cup unseasoned dry bread crumbs
1/3 cup finely chopped onion
1/4 cup ketchup or chili sauce
1 tablespoon lemon juice
1 teaspoon soy sauce
1 teaspoon Worcestershire sauce
1/8 teaspoon pepper
6 whole wheat burger buns, split

1. Heat gas or charcoal grill. In large bowl, mix all ingredients except buns. Shape mixture into 6 patties, 1/2 inch thick.

2. When grill is heated, lightly oil grill rack. Place patties on gas grill over medium heat or on charcoal grill over medium coals; cover grill. Cook 10 to 12 minutes, turning once, until patties are no longer pink and thermometer inserted in center of patties reads 165°F. Serve patties in buns.

1 Sandwich: Calories 240 (Calories from Fat 60); Total Fat 6g (Saturated Fat 1.5g; Trans Fat 0g); Cholesterol 50mg; Sodium 500mg; Total Carbohydrate 27g (Dietary Fiber 3g; Sugars 7g); Protein 21g
% Daily Value: Vitamin A 4%; Vitamin C 2%; Calcium 6%; Iron 15%
Exchanges: 1 1/2 Starch, 1/2 Other Carbohydrate, 2 Lean Meat
Carbohydrate Choices: 2

pacific northwest
salmon burgers

start to finish / **25 MINUTES**

5 sandwiches

6 whole grain burger buns, split

3/4 teaspoon grated lemon peel

2 tablespoons lemon juice

1 egg white

1 can (14.75 oz.) pink salmon, well drained, skin and large bones discarded, flaked

1/4 cup mayonnaise or salad dressing

2 tablespoons chopped fresh dill or 1 teaspoon dried dill weed

1 medium tomato, sliced

1/2 medium cucumber, thinly sliced

1. Heat gas or charcoal grill. Cut 1 burger bun into 1/2-inch cubes (1 1/2 cups); place in medium bowl. Add lemon peel, lemon juice and egg white; mix well. Stir in salmon. Shape mixture into 5 flat oval-shaped patties, 1/2 inch thick.

2. In small bowl, mix mayonnaise and dill; set aside.

3. When grill is heated, place patties on gas grill over medium-high heat or on charcoal grill over medium-high coals; cover grill. Cook 8 to 16 minutes, turning once, until patties are lightly browned on both sides.

4. To serve, spread cut sides of bun halves with mayonnaise mixture. Place patties on bottom halves of buns. Top with tomato and cucumber slices. Cover with top halves of buns.

1 Sandwich: Calories 230 (Calories from Fat 60); Total Fat 7g (Saturated Fat 2g; Trans Fat 0g); Cholesterol 45mg; Sodium 780mg; Total Carbohydrate 24g (Dietary Fiber 4g, Sugars 6g); Protein 21g
% Daily Value: Vitamin A 6%; Vitamin C 6%; Calcium 20%; Iron 15%
Exchanges: 1 Starch, 1/2 Other Carbohydrate, 2 1/2 Lean Meat
Carbohydrate Choices: 1 1/2

salads
on the side

These go-together-in-a-few-minutes sides can easily travel to a picnic site or wait while the meat, fish or chicken cooks on the grill.

warm honey mustard potato salad

Prep: 25 min

- 1 bag (24 oz.) frozen potato wedges with skins
- 1/4 cup honey
- 1/4 cup prepared yellow mustard
- 1 cup sliced celery (1 1/2 to 2 stalks)
- 1/2 medium red bell pepper, chopped (1/2 cup)
- 2 medium green onions, chopped (2 tablespoons) or red onion
- 1/4 teaspoon each garlic powder and salt
- 1/8 teaspoon coarsely ground black pepper

1. In 2-quart microwavable casserole, place potatoes; cover. Microwave on High 5 to 8 minutes or until desired doneness. Cool slightly, about 10 minutes.
2. Meanwhile, in small bowl, mix honey and mustard until well blended.
3. Cut potato wedges in half; return to casserole. Gently stir in celery, bell pepper, onions, garlic powder, salt and pepper. Pour honey mixture over potato mixture; stir gently until well coated.

12 servings (1/2 cup each)

fiesta corn salad

Prep: 15 min

- 1 bag (1 lb.) frozen whole kernel corn
- 1 can (15.5 or 15 oz.) kidney beans, drained, rinsed
- 1/2 cup chunky-style salsa
- 3 tablespoons each chopped green onions (3 medium) and chopped fresh cilantro
- 1/4 teaspoon each garlic powder and ground cumin

1. Cook corn as directed on bag.
2. In medium bowl, mix hot corn and remaining ingredients.

8 servings (1/2 cup each)

island fruit bowl

Prep: 25 min

- 1/4 cup flaked or shredded coconut
- 2 kiwifruit, peeled, sliced
- 1 mango, peeled, seeded and cut into chunks (about 1 cup)
- 1 can (20 oz.) pineapple chunks in juice, drained
- 2 cups sliced fresh strawberries
- 1 tablespoon chopped fresh cilantro
- 3/4 teaspoon ground ginger
- 1 cup frozen (thawed) fat-free whipped topping
- 1 container (4 oz.) vanilla fat-free pudding

1. Heat oven to 375°F. To toast coconut, place on cookie sheet or in pie pan. Bake 2 to 4 minutes, stirring occasionally, until golden brown.
2. In large bowl, gently mix all fruit, the cilantro and ginger. In small bowl, mix whipped topping and pudding until well blended. Add to fruit mixture; toss gently to mix thoroughly. Sprinkle with coconut.

6 servings (3/4 cup each)

warm honey mustard potato salad

california bean burgers

start to finish / **30 MINUTES**

6 sandwiches

"Eating bean patties topped with fresh veggies lets us splurge with a bit of guacamole. We like beans and know they have lots of fiber and other good-for-us things."

— Linc

2 cans (15.5 or 15 oz. each) red kidney beans, drained, rinsed
1/4 cup Italian-style dry bread crumbs
1 teaspoon Worcestershire sauce
2 medium green onions, chopped (2 tablespoons)
1 egg white
3 tablespoons sesame seed
12 slices sourdough bread
1/4 cup guacamole
1 medium carrot, shredded (3/4 cup)

1. Heat gas or charcoal grill. In food processor or large bowl with fork, process or mash beans until smooth. Add bread crumbs, Worcestershire sauce, onions and egg white; process with on/off pulses or stir until well combined.

2. Place sesame seed on plate. With wet hands, shape mixture into 6 flat oval-shaped patties, 1/2 inch thick. Coat patties evenly on both sides with seed.

3. When grill is heated, place patties on gas grill over medium-high heat or on charcoal grill over medium-high coals; cover grill. Cook 12 to 16 minutes, turning once, until patties are lightly browned on both sides and seed is toasted.

4. If desired, just before patties are done, place slices of bread on grill to toast lightly.

5. To serve, spread 1 side of each toasted slice of bread with 1 teaspoon guacamole. Top 6 slices of bread, guacamole side up, with patties. Top each with carrot. Cover with remaining bread slices, guacamole side down.

1 Sandwich: Calories 380 (Calories from Fat 60); Total Fat 7g (Saturated Fat 1.5g; Trans Fat 0g); Cholesterol 0mg; Sodium 490mg; Total Carbohydrate 67g (Dietary Fiber 11g; Sugars 3g); Protein 19g
% Daily Value: Vitamin A 50%; Vitamin C 6%; Calcium 10%; Iron 35%
Exchanges: 4 1/2 Starch, 1 Lean Meat
Carbohydrate Choices: 4

california bean burgers

milanese beef grill SUPER EXPRESS

start to finish **/ 20 MINUTES**

4 servings

1 lb. boneless beef top round steak
  (3/4 inch thick)
1/4 teaspoon salt
1/8 to 1/4 teaspoon pepper
1/3 cup finely chopped fresh parsley
2 tablespoons grated lemon peel
3 large cloves garlic, minced
1/4 cup dry white wine or chicken
  broth
1 tablespoon Dijon mustard

1. Heat gas or charcoal grill. Lightly sprinkle both sides of steak with salt and pepper.

2. When grill is heated, place steak on gas grill over medium heat or on charcoal grill over medium coals; cover grill. Cook 8 to 11 minutes, turning once, until desired doneness.

3. Meanwhile, in shallow dish, mix remaining ingredients.

4. Remove steak from grill; cut diagonally across grain into slices. Coat each slice with sauce mixture before placing on individual plates. Spoon any remaining sauce over steak slices.

1 Serving: Calories 130 (Calories from Fat 35); Total Fat 4g (Saturated Fat 1g; Trans Fat 0g); Cholesterol 60mg; Sodium 290mg; Total Carbohydrate 2g (Dietary Fiber 0g; Sugars 0g); Protein 23g
% Daily Value: Vitamin A 10%; Vitamin C 10%; Calcium 2%; Iron 15%
Exchanges: 3 Very Lean Meat, 1/2 Fat
Carbohydrate Choices: 0

beef and
vegetable packets

4 servings

> *"There's nothing easier than adding a purchased sauce to my fresh meat and veggies. This is a great all-family meal, and my kids love it because they get their own individual packets. I know they'll ask for this again and again."*
>
> — *Maria*

4 medium potatoes, thinly sliced (4 cups)
8 large mushrooms, sliced (2 cups)
4 large carrots, thinly sliced (2 cups)
2 medium onions, sliced
1/2 lb. extra-lean (at least 90%) ground beef
1 cup barbecue sauce

1. Heat gas or charcoal grill. Cut 4 (20 x 18-inch) sheets of heavy-duty foil. Fold each in half to form 18 x 10-inch rectangle.

2. In large bowl, mix potatoes, mushrooms, carrots and onions. Crumble ground beef over vegetables. Add barbecue sauce; toss until well coated. Spoon 1/4 of mixture onto each sheet of foil. Wrap each packet securely using double-fold seals, allowing room for heat expansion.

3. When grill is heated, place packets on gas grill over medium heat or on charcoal grill over medium coals; cover grill. Cook 20 minutes, turning packets over once, until vegetables are tender and beef is brown. Carefully open packets to allow steam to escape.

1 Serving: Calories 340 (Calories from Fat 45); Total Fat 5g (Saturated Fat 2g; Trans Fat 0g); Cholesterol 35mg; Sodium 680mg; Total Carbohydrate 61g (Dietary Fiber 7g; Sugars 24g); Protein 16g
% Daily Value: Vitamin A 230%; Vitamin C 25%; Calcium 8%; Iron 30%
Exchanges: 1 1/2 Starch, 2 1/2 Other Carbohydrate, 1 1/2 Lean Meat
Carbohydrate Choices: 3 1/2

pork with
tropical
fruit kabobs

start to finish **/ 25 MINUTES**

6 servings

2 tablespoons pineapple juice

1/2 teaspoon soy sauce

1 teaspoon liquid smoke

6 boneless pork loin chops, 1/2 inch thick (1 lb.)

6 skewers (10 inch)

2 large firm ripe bananas, cut into 3-inch pieces

12 chunks fresh or canned pineapple

1 medium red bell pepper, seeded, cut into 1-inch squares

1/2 red onion, cut into 1 1/2-inch pieces

3 tablespoons rum, or 1 tablespoon rum extract plus 2 tablespoons water

3 tablespoons honey

1. In resealable plastic food-storage bag or shallow dish, mix pineapple juice, soy sauce and liquid smoke. Place pork in bag in single layer, rubbing mixture well into both sides of pork. Let stand at room temperature 10 minutes to marinate.

2. Meanwhile, heat gas or charcoal grill. On each skewer, thread banana, pineapple, bell pepper and onion pieces. In small bowl, mix rum and honey. Brush mixture over kabobs, reserving some of mixture to brush on kabobs during grilling.

3. When grill is heated, place pork and kabobs on gas grill over medium heat or on charcoal grill over medium coals; cover grill. Cook 6 to 8 minutes, turning and brushing kabobs with rum mixture once halfway through cooking, until pork is slightly pink in center and kabobs are hot.

1 Serving: Calories 230 (Calories from Fat 60); Total Fat 6g (Saturated Fat 2g; Trans Fat 0g); Cholesterol 45mg; Sodium 55mg; Total Carbohydrate 27g (Dietary Fiber 2g; Sugars 20g); Protein 17g
% Daily Value: Vitamin A 25%; Vitamin C 40%; Calcium 0%; Iron 6%
Exchanges: 1 Fruit, 1 Other Carbohydrate, 2 1/2 Very Lean Meat, 1/2 Fat
Carbohydrate Choices: 2

summer
pork kabobs

start to finish / **30 MINUTES**

4 servings

4 boneless pork loin chops,
   3/4 inch thick (1 lb.)

1/2 teaspoon seasoned salt or
   dried pork seasoning

2 small zucchini, cut into
   12 (1-inch) pieces

8 medium mushrooms

1 medium red bell pepper, cut
   into 12 pieces

1/2 cup apricot preserves

1 tablespoon cider vinegar

1. Heat gas or charcoal grill. Sprinkle pork chops with seasoned salt; cut each chop into 4 pieces. Alternately thread pork pieces, zucchini, mushrooms and bell pepper equally onto each of 4 (12- to 14-inch) metal skewers. In small bowl, mix preserves and vinegar.

2. When grill is heated, place kabobs on gas grill over medium heat or on charcoal grill over medium coals. Brush kabobs with preserves mixture; cover grill. Cook 5 to 7 minutes. Turn kabobs; brush with preserves mixture. Cook covered 5 to 7 minutes longer or until pork is no longer pink in center.

1 Serving: Calories 310 (Calories from Fat 80); Total Fat 9g (Saturated Fat 3g; Trans Fat 0g); Cholesterol 70mg; Sodium 230mg; Total Carbohydrate 33g (Dietary Fiber 2g; Sugars 22g); Protein 26g
% Daily Value: Vitamin A 45%; Vitamin C 60%; Calcium 2%; Iron 10%
Exchanges: 2 Other Carbohydrate, 1 Vegetable, 3 1/2 Lean Meat
Carbohydrate Choices: 2

easy italian
spiced pork

start to finish **/ 30 MINUTES**

4 servings

1 package (0.6 oz.) Italian dressing mix
1/4 cup balsamic vinegar
1/2 teaspoon Italian seasoning
1/4 teaspoon crushed red pepper
1 tablespoon extra-virgin olive oil or canola oil
4 boneless pork loin chops, 3/4 inch thick (1 lb.)
Paprika

1. In small bowl, beat dressing mix, vinegar, Italian seasoning and red pepper with wire whisk until mix is dissolved. Beat in oil until well blended.

2. In shallow glass baking dish, arrange pork chops in single layer. Spread oil mixture over both sides of pork. Let stand at room temperature 15 minutes to marinate.

3. Meanwhile, heat gas or charcoal grill.

4. When grill is heated, remove pork from marinade; discard marinade. Place pork on gas grill over medium-high heat or on charcoal grill over medium-high coals. Sprinkle pork with paprika. Cook uncovered 4 minutes. Turn pork; sprinkle with paprika. Cook uncovered 3 to 6 minutes longer or until pork is slightly pink in center and thermometer inserted in center of pork reads 160°F.

1 Serving: Calories 220 (Calories from Fat 110); Total Fat 12g (Saturated Fat 3.5g; Trans Fat 0g); Cholesterol 70mg; Sodium 680mg; Total Carbohydrate 4g (Dietary Fiber 0g; Sugars 3g); Protein 24g
% Daily Value: Vitamin A 4%; Vitamin C 0%; Calcium 0%; Iron 6%
Exchanges: 1/2 Other Carbohydrate, 3 1/2 Lean Meat
Carbohydrate Choices: 0

pork-pineapple kabobs with
plum-ginger glaze

start to finish **/ 40 MINUTES**

4 servings

1 lb. pork tenderloin, cut into 1-inch pieces
3 tablespoons reduced-sodium soy sauce
1/3 cup plum sauce
2 teaspoons grated orange peel
1 teaspoon grated gingerroot
1/4 teaspoon crushed red pepper
16 green onions
4 fresh pineapple spears (6 inch)
Hot cooked instant rice, if desired

1. In resealable plastic food-storage bag or 13 x 9-inch (3-quart) glass baking dish, place pork pieces. Pour soy sauce over pork; toss to coat. Seal bag or cover dish. Let stand at room temperature 15 minutes to marinate, turning or stirring occasionally.

2. Meanwhile, heat gas or charcoal grill. In small bowl, mix plum sauce, orange peel, gingerroot and red pepper; set aside. Cut green onions into 1-inch pieces. Cut each pineapple spear into 6 pieces.

3. Alternately thread pork, onion (skewered crosswise) and pineapple evenly onto 4 (12- to 15-inch) metal skewers; discard marinade.

4. When grill is heated, carefully oil grill rack; place kabobs on gas grill over medium-high heat or on charcoal grill over medium-high coals. Brush plum sauce mixture over kabobs; cover grill. Cook 5 minutes. Turn kabobs; brush with sauce mixture. Cook covered 4 to 6 minutes longer, brushing frequently with sauce mixture, until pork is no longer pink in center. Discard any remaining sauce. If desired, serve with hot cooked instant white and wild rice.

1 Serving: Calories 230 (Calories from Fat 45); Total Fat 5g (Saturated Fat 1.5g; Trans Fat 0g); Cholesterol 70mg; Sodium 460mg; Total Carbohydrate 21g (Dietary Fiber 3g; Sugars 14g); Protein 28g
% Daily Value: Vitamin A 10%; Vitamin C 20%; Calcium 6%; Iron 15%
Exchanges: 1/2 Fruit, 1 Other Carbohydrate, 4 Very Lean Meat
Carbohydrate Choices: 1 1/2

pork with
sweet-spiced
caribbean rub SUPER EXPRESS

start to finish / 20 MINUTES

4 servings

"The sweet-hot seasoning gives the pork chops the flavor associated with the term 'jerk.' Grilled fresh pineapple spears would add another tropical flavor."

—Sally

1 tablespoon packed dark brown sugar
1 teaspoon ground ginger
1 1/2 teaspoons ground allspice
1 teaspoon ground cinnamon
1/2 teaspoon dried thyme leaves
1/4 teaspoon salt
1/4 teaspoon ground red pepper (cayenne)
1/8 teaspoon ground cloves
4 boneless pork loin chops, 1/2 inch thick (about 3/4 lb.)
2 teaspoons olive or canola oil

1. Heat gas or charcoal grill. In small bowl, mix all ingredients except pork chops and oil until well blended. Place pork on large plate; spoon 1/4 teaspoon oil on each side of pork. Sprinkle about 1 teaspoon spice mixture over each side. With fingers, rub into pork.

2. When grill is heated, place pork on gas grill over medium-high heat or on charcoal grill over medium-high coals. Cook uncovered 8 to 10 minutes, turning once, until pork is browned and slightly pink in center.

1 Serving: Calories 170 (Calories from Fat 80); Total Fat 9g (Saturated Fat 2.5g; Trans Fat 0g); Cholesterol 50mg; Sodium 180mg; Total Carbohydrate 5g (Dietary Fiber 0g; Sugars 3g); Protein 18g
% Daily Value: Vitamin A 0%; Vitamin C 0%; Calcium 2%; Iron 6%
Exchanges: 1/2 Other Carbohydrate, 2 1/2 Lean Meat, 1/2 Fat
Carbohydrate Choices: 1/2

mustard-glazed
pork chops

start to finish **/ 25 MINUTES**

6 servings

"As long as I have the grill fired up, I'd rather make the whole meal on it. I'd serve these tangy chops with grilled potato or sweet potato wedges, then I'd add a tossed salad."

—Ben

2 tablespoons packed brown sugar
1 teaspoon onion powder
1/4 cup beer or ginger ale
2 tablespoons prepared yellow mustard
1 tablespoon canola or soybean oil
1 tablespoon soy sauce
6 boneless pork loin chops, 3/4 inch thick (1 1/2 lb.)

1. Heat gas or charcoal grill. In small bowl, mix brown sugar and onion powder. Stir in beer, mustard, oil and soy sauce until well blended.

2. When grill is heated, place pork chops on gas grill over medium heat or on charcoal grill over medium coals; cover grill. Cook 10 to 15 minutes, turning and brushing once or twice with mustard mixture, until pork is slightly pink in center and thermometer inserted in center of pork reads 160°F.

1 Serving: Calories 220 (Calories from Fat 100); Total Fat 11g (Saturated Fat 3g; Trans Fat 0g); Cholesterol 70mg; Sodium 250mg; Total Carbohydrate 5g (Dietary Fiber 0g; Sugars 5g); Protein 25g
% Daily Value: Vitamin A 0%; Vitamin C 0%; Calcium 0%; Iron 6%
Exchanges: 1/2 Other Carbohydrate, 3 1/2 Lean Meat
Carbohydrate Choices: 1/2

honey-orange glazed pork chops

start to finish / **25 MINUTES**

4 servings

> *"I look for easy recipes with only a few ingredients that I have on hand and those that my family will like. This one fits on all levels."*
> — *Carlos*

4 boneless pork loin chops, 3/4 inch thick (1 lb.)
3 tablespoons Worcestershire sauce
1/3 cup honey
1 tablespoon grated orange peel
1/4 teaspoon salt

1. In shallow glass baking dish, place pork chops. Brush 1 tablespoon Worcestershire sauce over both sides of each. Let stand at room temperature 15 minutes to marinate.

2. Meanwhile, heat gas or charcoal grill. In 2-quart saucepan, mix remaining 2 tablespoons Worcestershire sauce, the honey, orange peel and salt until well blended. Heat to boiling over high heat. Reduce heat to medium; boil 1 minute.

3. When grill is heated, place pork on gas grill over medium-high heat or on charcoal grill over medium-high coals. Spoon half of honey mixture evenly over pork. Cook uncovered 5 minutes. Turn pork; spoon remaining honey mixture over pork. Cook uncovered 3 to 5 minutes longer or until pork is slightly pink in center and thermometer inserted in center of pork reads 160°F.

1 Serving: Calories 280 (Calories from Fat 80); Total Fat 9g (Saturated Fat 3g; Trans Fat 0g); Cholesterol 70mg; Sodium 320mg; Total Carbohydrate 26g (Dietary Fiber 0g; Sugars 25g); Protein 24g
% Daily Value: Vitamin A 0%; Vitamin C 4%; Calcium 2%; Iron 10%
Exchanges: 1 1/2 Other Carbohydrate, 3 1/2 Lean Meat
Carbohydrate Choices: 2

honey-orange glazed pork chops

corn, pork and bean
bundles

4 servings

3/4 lb. boneless pork loin chops, cut into 2 x 1/4-inch strips
1 can (15 oz.) red beans, rinsed
1/2 cup barbecue sauce
1 cup frozen whole kernel corn (from 1-lb. bag), thawed
4 thin slices onion

1. Heat gas or charcoal grill. Cut 4 (15 x 12-inch) sheets of foil. In medium bowl, mix pork, beans and barbecue sauce. Divide pork mixture evenly onto center of each sheet of foil. Sprinkle corn evenly over top. Place onion slice on top of each.

2. To form bundles, bring short sides of foil together; make several 1-inch folds. Fold open edges of foil to seal.

3. When grill is heated, place bundles on gas grill over medium heat or on charcoal grill over medium coals; cover grill. Cook 18 to 20 minutes or until pork is no longer pink in center. Carefully open bundles to allow steam to escape.

1 Serving: Calories 340 (Calories from Fat 60); Total Fat 7g (Saturated Fat 2.5g; Trans Fat 0g); Cholesterol 50mg; Sodium 350mg; Total Carbohydrate 44g (Dietary Fiber 8g; Sugars 10g); Protein 29g
% Daily Value: Vitamin A 4%; Vitamin C 4%; Calcium 4%; Iron 25%
Exchanges: 2 Starch, 1 Other Carbohydrate, 3 Very Lean Meat, 1/2 Fat
Carbohydrate Choices: 2 1/2

sausage and veggie pitas

4 servings (2 sandwiches each)

> "We use our grill all year-round, and we all love these tasty filled pitas. When I make them, I separate each pita bread into two rounds, then spoon the filling onto the rounds and form them into cone-shaped wraps."
>
> —Kevin

2 teaspoons sugar
3 tablespoons Worcestershire sauce
1 medium yellow summer squash, cut lengthwise into 1/2-inch-thick slices
1 medium zucchini, cut lengthwise into 1/2-inch-thick slices
1 medium red or green bell pepper, halved, seeded
1 medium yellow onion, cut into 1/2-inch-thick slices
1/2 lb. 95%-fat-free turkey kielbasa
4 onion or plain pita breads (6 inch), cut in half to form pockets, heated
1 tablespoon extra-virgin olive oil or canola oil

1. Heat gas or charcoal grill. In small bowl, mix sugar and Worcestershire sauce until sugar is dissolved. Brush half of mixture over summer squash, zucchini, bell pepper, onion and kielbasa.

2. When grill is heated, carefully oil grill rack. Place vegetables and kielbasa on gas grill over medium-high heat or on charcoal grill over medium-high coals; cover grill. Cook 6 minutes. Turn vegetables and kielbasa; brush with remaining mixture. Cook on open grill 4 to 6 minutes longer or until vegetables are tender and kielbasa is hot.

3. To heat pita bread halves, wrap in foil; place on grill 3 to 5 minutes or until warm.

4. Remove vegetables and kielbasa from grill. Cut into bite-size pieces; place in serving bowl. Add oil; toss to mix. Fill warm pita bread halves evenly with vegetables and kielbasa.

1 Serving: Calories 300 (Calories from Fat 80); Total Fat 9g (Saturated Fat 2g; Trans Fat 0g); Cholesterol 30mg; Sodium 970mg; Total Carbohydrate 41g (Dietary Fiber 4g; Sugars 9g); Protein 15g
% Daily Value: Vitamin A 45%; Vitamin C 60%; Calcium 10%; Iron 15%
Exchanges: 2 Starch, 1/2 Other Carbohydrate, 1 Vegetable, 1 Medium-Fat Meat, 1/2 Fat
Carbohydrate Choices: 3

chicken with caramelized onion glaze

start to finish / **40 MINUTES**

4 servings

1/2 cup raspberry spreadable fruit
1 1/2 teaspoons grated gingerroot
1 tablespoon red wine vinegar
1 tablespoon soy sauce
2 teaspoons canola or soybean oil
1 medium onion, chopped (1/2 cup)
4 bone-in chicken breasts, skin removed

1. Heat gas or charcoal grill. In small bowl, beat raspberry spreadable fruit, gingerroot, vinegar and soy sauce with wire whisk until well blended; set aside.

2. In 10-inch nonstick skillet, heat oil over high heat 1 minute. Add onion; cook and stir 2 minutes. Reduce heat to medium; cook 2 minutes longer or until onion is tender and rich dark brown. Reduce heat to low; stir in raspberry mixture. Cook 1 minute, stirring constantly. Remove from heat; set aside.

3. When grill is heated, place chicken, bone side up, on gas grill over medium-high heat or on charcoal grill over medium-high coals; cover grill. Cook 15 to 17 minutes, turning frequently, until juice of chicken is no longer pink when centers of thickest part is cut to bone (170°F). Spoon onion-raspberry mixture over meaty side of chicken; cook uncovered 2 minutes longer.

1 Serving: Calories 270 (Calories from Fat 60); Total Fat 7g (Saturated Fat 1.5g; Trans Fat 0g); Cholesterol 75mg; Sodium 300mg; Total Carbohydrate 26g (Dietary Fiber 3g; Sugars 21g); Protein 28g
% Daily Value: Vitamin A 2%; Vitamin C 4%; Calcium 4%; Iron 8%
Exchanges: 1 1/2 Other Carbohydrate, 4 Very Lean Meat, 1 Fat
Carbohydrate Choices: 2

chicken with caramelized onion glaze

cajun chicken with fresh tomato relish SUPER EXPRESS

start to finish / **20 MINUTES**

4 servings

Relish
2 medium tomatoes, chopped (about 1 1/2 cups)
8 medium green onions, chopped (1/2 cup)
1/3 cup chopped celery
1/4 teaspoon salt
1/4 teaspoon red pepper sauce

Chicken
4 boneless, skinless chicken breasts (about 1 lb.)
3 teaspoons Cajun seasoning

1. In medium bowl, mix relish ingredients; set aside. Heat gas or charcoal grill. Coat both sides of each chicken breast evenly with Cajun seasoning.

2. When grill is heated, carefully oil grill rack. Place chicken on gas grill over medium heat or on charcoal grill over medium coals; cover grill. Cook 10 minutes, turning once, until juice of chicken is no longer pink when center of thickest part is cut (170°F). Serve chicken with relish.

1 Serving: Calories 150 (Calories from Fat 35); Total Fat 4g (Saturated Fat 1g; Trans Fat 0g); Cholesterol 70mg; Sodium 630mg; Total Carbohydrate 4g (Dietary Fiber 1g; Sugars 2g); Protein 26g
% Daily Value: Vitamin A 15%; Vitamin C 15%; Calcium 2%; Iron 8%
Exchanges: 1 Vegetable, 3 1/2 Very Lean Meat, 1/2 Fat
Carbohydrate Choices: 0

grilled
swordfish

4 servings

1 tablespoon olive or canola oil
1/3 cup finely chopped shallots
1 tablespoon finely chopped fresh thyme
1/2 teaspoon sugar
1/2 teaspoon grated lemon peel
2 tablespoons Dijon mustard
2 tablespoons white wine or water
2 lb. swordfish steaks, cut into 6 serving-size pieces

1. Heat gas or charcoal grill. In 7-inch nonstick skillet, heat oil over medium heat. Add shallots; cook 3 minutes, stirring frequently, until tender. Remove from heat. Stir in thyme, sugar, lemon peel, mustard and wine until well blended. Spread half of mixture on one side of swordfish pieces.

2. When grill is heated, carefully oil grill rack. Place fish, spread side up, on gas grill over medium heat or on charcoal grill over medium coals; cover grill. Cook 6 minutes. Turn fish; spread remaining shallot mixture over fish. Cook 5 to 7 minutes longer or until fish flakes easily with fork.

1 Serving: Calories 200 (Calories from Fat 90); Total Fat 9g (Saturated Fat 2.5g; Trans Fat 0g); Cholesterol 80mg; Sodium 200mg; Total Carbohydrate 2g (Dietary Fiber 0g; Sugars 0g); Protein 26g
% Daily Value: Vitamin A 4%; Vitamin C 4%; Calcium 2%; Iron 6%
Exchanges: 3 1/2 Lean Meat
Carbohydrate Choices: 0

swordfish with
pineapple salsa

6 servings

"If I can't get swordfish, I might use another firm-textured fish, such as grouper, halibut, shark or tuna."

—Donna

Salsa
1/2 medium fresh pineapple, rind removed, cored and finely chopped
1 red bell pepper, seeded, finely chopped
1 jalapeño chili, seeded, finely chopped
1 clove garlic, minced
3/4 cup finely chopped red onion
1/4 cup chopped fresh cilantro

Swordfish
1/2 cup pineapple juice
1 tablespoon grated lime peel
2 tablespoons lime juice
2 tablespoons rum, if desired
1 tablespoon olive or canola oil
1 teaspoon paprika or 1/4 teaspoon ground red pepper (cayenne)
2 lb. swordfish steaks, cut into 6 serving-size pieces

1. In medium bowl, mix salsa ingredients. Refrigerate until serving time or up to 4 days.

2. Heat gas or charcoal grill. In shallow dish, mix pineapple juice, lime peel, lime juice, rum, if desired, the oil and paprika. Place swordfish in dish; let stand at room temperature 10 minutes to marinate.

3. When grill is heated, place fish on gas grill over medium heat or on charcoal grill over medium coals; cover grill. Cook 8 to 12 minutes, turning once, until fish flakes easily with fork. Serve fish with salsa.

1 Serving: Calories 230 (Calories from Fat 90); Total Fat 9g (Saturated Fat 2.5g; Trans Fat 0g); Cholesterol 80mg; Sodium 75mg; Total Carbohydrate 12g (Dietary Fiber 2g; Sugars 9g); Protein 26g
% Daily Value: Vitamin A 35%; Vitamin C 90%; Calcium 4%; Iron 8%
Exchanges: 1/2 Fruit, 1/2 Other Carbohydrate, 3 1/2 Lean Meat
Carbohydrate Choices: 1

swordfish with pineapple salsa

grilled
marinated shrimp

start to finish / **30 MINUTES**

4 servings

"My kids love shrimp, and I'm always looking for new, easy ways to cook it. This is a great easy recipe because cleanup is at a minimum."

—Cheri

1/2 teaspoon grated lime peel

1/4 teaspoon ground cumin

1/4 teaspoon dried oregano leaves

1/8 teaspoon salt

2 tablespoons olive or canola oil

2 tablespoons lime juice

2 cloves garlic, minced

1 lb. uncooked peeled deveined large shrimp

1. Heat gas or charcoal grill. In medium bowl, mix all ingredients except shrimp. Add shrimp; toss to coat. Let stand at room temperature 10 minutes to marinate.

2. Remove shrimp from marinade; thread loosely onto 4 (12- to 14-inch) metal skewers. Reserve marinade.

3. When ready to grill, place skewered shrimp on gas grill over medium heat or on charcoal grill over medium coals; cover grill. Cook 3 to 7 minutes, turning once and brushing occasionally with reserved marinade, until shrimp turn pink. Discard any remaining marinade.

1 Serving: Calories 140 (Calories from Fat 70); Total Fat 8g (Saturated Fat 1g; Trans Fat 0g); Cholesterol 160mg; Sodium 260mg; Total Carbohydrate 1g (Dietary Fiber 0g; Sugars 0g); Protein 17g
% Daily Value: Vitamin A 6%; Vitamin C 4%; Calcium 4%; Iron 15%
Exchanges: 2 1/2 Very Lean Meat, 1 1/2 Fat
Carbohydrate Choices: 0

grilled marinated shrimp

pineapple-glazed
chicken breasts

start to finish **/ 30 MINUTES**

4 servings

1/4 cup Dijon mustard
1/4 cup frozen (thawed) pineapple juice concentrate
2 cloves garlic, minced
2 tablespoons chopped fresh rosemary or 1 teaspoon dried rosemary leaves
1/2 teaspoon salt
1/4 teaspoon pepper
4 boneless, skinless chicken breast halves (5 oz. each)
2 teaspoons olive oil
4 slices (1/2 inch thick) fresh pineapple, rind removed

1. Heat gas or charcoal grill. In small bowl, mix mustard and juice concentrate; reserve 2 tablespoons. Into remaining mixture, stir garlic, rosemary, salt and pepper; set aside.

2. When grill is heated, rub chicken breast halves with oil. Place chicken on gas grill over medium heat or on charcoal grill over medium coals; cover grill. Cook 5 minutes.

3. Add pineapple to grill; brush with rosemary mixture. Turn chicken; brush with rosemary mixture. Cover grill; cook 6 to 8 minutes longer, brushing chicken occasionally with rosemary mixture and turning chicken and pineapple once, until chicken is fork-tender and juice is no longer pink when centers of thickest pieces are cut. Discard any remaining rosemary mixture.

4. Place chicken on serving plates. Spoon reserved 2 tablespoons mustard mixture over chicken. Halve or quarter pineapple slices; serve with chicken.

1 Serving: Calories 270 (Calories from Fat: 70); Total Fat 8g 12% (Saturated Fat 1.5g; Trans Fat 0g); Cholesterol 85mg; Sodium 750mg; Total Carbohydrate 17g (Dietary Fiber 1g; Sugars 12g); Protein 32g
% Daily Value: Vitamin A 2%; Vitamin C 15%; Calcium 4%; Iron 10%
Exchanges: 1 Fruit, 4 1/2 Very Lean Meat, 1 Fat
Carbohydrate Choices: 1

fiesta quesadillas SUPER EXPRESS

start to finish / **15 MINUTES**

6 servings

1 can (11 oz.) whole kernel corn with red and green peppers, drained
1 can (16 oz.) fat-free refried beans
6 flour tortillas (8 to 10 inch)
1 cup shredded colby-Monterey Jack cheese blend (4 oz.)

1. Heat gas or charcoal grill. In medium bowl, mix corn and refried beans. Spread mixture evenly onto 3 tortillas. Top with remaining tortillas.

2. When grill is heated, place filled tortillas on gas grill over low heat or on charcoal grill over low coals; cover grill. Cook 5 minutes. With pancake turner, carefully turn tortillas; sprinkle with cheese. Cook 3 to 5 minutes longer or until cheese is melted. Cut into wedges to serve.

1 Serving: Calories 300 (Calories from Fat 80); Total Fat 9g (Saturated Fat 4.5g; Trans Fat 0.5g); Cholesterol 20mg; Sodium 590mg; Total Carbohydrate 45g (Dietary Fiber 6g; Sugars 2g); Protein 13g
% Daily Value: Vitamin A 6%; Vitamin C 6%; Calcium 20%; Iron 15%
Exchanges: 3 Starch, 1/2 Very Lean Meat, 1 Fat
Carbohydrate Choices: 2 1/2

helpful nutrition and
cooking information

Nutrition Guidelines

We provide nutrition information for each recipe that includes calories, fat, cholesterol, sodium, carbohydrate, fiber and protein. Individual food choices can be based on this information.

Recommended intake for a daily diet of 2,000 calories as set by the Food and Drug Administration

Total Fat	Less than 65g
Saturated Fat	Less than 20g
Cholesterol	Less than 300mg
Sodium	Less than 2,400mg
Total Carbohydrate	300g
Dietary Fiber	25g

Criteria Used for Calculating Nutrition Information

- The first ingredient was used wherever a choice is given (such as 1/3 cup sour cream or plain yogurt).

- The first ingredient amount was used wherever a range is given (such as 3 to 3 1/2 pounds cut-up broiler-fryer chicken).

- The first serving number was used wherever a range is given (such as 4 to 6 servings).

- "If desired" ingredients and recipe variations were not included (such as sprinkle with brown sugar, if desired).

- Only the amount of a marinade or frying oil that is estimated to be absorbed by the food during preparation or cooking was calculated.

Ingredients Used in Recipe Testing and Nutrition Calculations

- Ingredients used for testing represent those that the majority of consumers use in their homes: large eggs, 2% milk, 80%-lean ground beef, canned ready-to-use chicken broth and vegetable oil spread containing not less than 65 percent fat.

- Fat-free, low-fat or low-sodium products were not used, unless otherwise indicated.

- Solid vegetable shortening (not butter, margarine, nonstick cooking sprays or vegetable oil spread as they can cause sticking problems) was used to grease pans, unless otherwise indicated.

Equipment Used in Recipe Testing

- We use equipment for testing that the majority of consumers use in their homes. If a specific piece of equipment (such as a wire whisk) is necessary for recipe success, it is listed in the recipe.

- Cookware and bakeware without nonstick coatings were used, unless otherwise indicated.

- No dark-colored, black or insulated bakeware was used.

- When a pan is specified in a recipe, a metal pan was used; a baking dish or pie plate means ovenproof glass was used.

- An electric hand mixer was used for mixing only when mixer speeds are specified in the recipe directions. When a mixer speed is not given, a spoon or fork was used.

Cooking Terms Glossary

Beat
Mix ingredients vigorously with spoon, fork, wire whisk, hand beater or electric mixer until smooth and uniform.

Boil
Heat liquid until bubbles rise continuously and break on the surface and steam is given off. For rolling boil, the bubbles form rapidly.

Chop
Cut into coarse or fine irregular pieces with a knife, food chopper, blender or food processor.

Cube
Cut into squares 1/2 inch or larger.

Dice
Cut into squares smaller than 1/2 inch.

Grate
Cut into tiny particles using small rough holes of grater (citrus peel or chocolate).

Grease
Rub the inside surface of a pan with shortening, using pastry brush, piece of waxed paper or paper towel, to prevent food from sticking during baking (as for some casseroles).

Julienne
Cut into thin, matchlike strips, using knife or food processor (vegetables, fruits, meats).

Mix
Combine ingredients in any way that distributes them evenly.

Sauté
Cook foods in hot oil or margarine over medium-high heat with frequent tossing and turning motion.

Shred
Cut into long thin pieces by rubbing food across the holes of a shredder, as for cheese, or by using a knife to slice very thinly, as for cabbage.

Simmer
Cook in liquid just below the boiling point on top of the stove; usually after reducing heat from a boil. Bubbles will rise slowly and break just below the surface.

Stir
Mix ingredients until uniform consistency. Stir once in a while for stirring occasionally, often for stirring frequently and continuously for stirring constantly.

Toss
Tumble ingredients (such as green salad) lightly with a lifting motion, usually to coat evenly or mix with another food.

metric conversion guide

volume

U.S. Units	Canadian Metric	Australian Metric
1/4 teaspoon	1 mL	1 ml
1/2 teaspoon	2 mL	2 ml
1 teaspoon	5 mL	5 ml
1 tablespoon	15 mL	20 ml
1/4 cup	50 mL	60 ml
1/3 cup	75 mL	80 ml
1/2 cup	125 mL	125 ml
2/3 cup	150 mL	170 ml
3/4 cup	175 mL	190 ml
1 cup	250 mL	250 ml
1 quart	1 liter	1 liter
1 1/2 quarts	1.5 liters	1.5 liters
2 quarts	2 liters	2 liters
2 1/2 quarts	2.5 liters	2.5 liters
3 quarts	3 liters	3 liters
4 quarts	4 liters	4 liters

weight

U.S. Units	Canadian Metric	Australian Metric
1 ounce	30 grams	30 grams
2 ounces	55 grams	60 grams
3 ounces	85 grams	90 grams
4 ounces (1/4 pound)	115 grams	125 grams
8 ounces (1/2 pound)	225 grams	225 grams
16 ounces (1 pound)	455 grams	500 grams
1 pound	455 grams	1/2 kilogram

measurements

Inches	Centimeters
1	2.5
2	5.0
3	7.5
4	10.0
5	12.5
6	15.0
7	17.5
8	20.5
9	23.0
10	25.5
11	28.0
12	30.5
13	33.0

temperatures

Fahrenheit	Celsius
32°	0°
212°	100°
250°	120°
275°	140°
300°	150°
325°	160°
350°	180°
375°	190°
400°	200°
425°	220°
450°	230°
475°	240°
500°	260°

Note: The recipes in this cookbook have not been developed or tested using metric measures. When converting recipes to metric, some variations in quality may be noted.

index

Page numbers in italics indicate illustrations.

(*continues*)

(continues)